DO-IT-YOURSELF
WEB PUBLISHING
WITH WORD

Do-It-Yourself
Web Publishing
with Word

Asha Dornfest

SYBEX

San Francisco • Paris • Düsseldorf • Soest

Associate Publisher: Carrie Lavine
Acquisitions and Developmental Editor: Brenda Kienan
Editor: Valerie Potter
Technical Editor: Kevin Horst
Production Coordinator: Alexa Riggs
Desktop Publisher: Bob Bihlmayer of London Road Design
Proofreader: Vicki Wilhite of London Road Design
Book Designer: Jan Haseman of London Road Design
Technical Artist: Cuong Le
Indexer: Linda Facey
Cover Designer: Design Site
Cover Illustrator: Jack D. Myers

Library of Congress Card Number: 95-72873
ISBN: 0-7821-1807-0

Manufactured in the United States of America
10 9 8 7 6 5 4 3 2 1

Warranty

Internet Assistant was reproduced by SYBEX Inc. under a special arrangement with Microsoft Corporation. For this reason, SYBEX is responsible for the product warranty and for support. SYBEX warrants the enclosed CD-ROM to be free of physical defects for a period of ninety (90) days after purchase. If you discover a defect in the CD during this warranty period, you can obtain a replacement CD at no charge by sending the defective CD, postage prepaid, with proof of purchase to:

SYBEX Inc.
Customer Service Department
2021 Challenger Drive
Alameda, CA 94501
(800) 227-2346
Fax: (510) 523-2373

PLEASE DO NOT RETURN A DEFECTIVE CD TO MICROSOFT CORPORATION.

After the 90-day period, you can obtain a replacement CD by sending us the defective CD, proof of purchase, and a check or money order for $10, payable to SYBEX.

Disclaimers

End users of this Microsoft program shall not be considered "registered owners" of a Microsoft product and therefore shall not be eligible for upgrades, promotions or other benefits available to "registered owners" of Microsoft products.

SYBEX makes no warranty or representation, either express or implied, with respect to this medium or its contents, its quality, performance, merchantability, or fitness for a particular purpose. In no event will SYBEX, its distributors, or dealers be liable for direct, indirect, special, incidental, or consequential damages arising out of the use of or inability to use the software even if advised of the possibility of such damage.

The exclusion of implied warranties is not permitted by some states. Therefore, the above exclusion may not apply to you. This warranty provides you with specific legal rights; there may be other rights that you may have that vary from state to state.

Copy Protection

None of the files on the CD is copy-protected. However, in all cases, reselling or making copies of these files without authorization is expressly forbidden.

*To Web publishers everywhere
who aspire to make their voices heard*

ACKNOWLEDGMENTS

I am lucky to be part of a remarkable team of people who worked together to create this book.

My heartfelt thanks go to Brenda Kienan, my developmental and acquisitions editor. I admire her editorial skill as well as the grace with which she tackled the snags that are an inevitable part of writing a computer book. It was a pleasure to work with my editor, Val Potter, who is incredibly dedicated to her work and is never too busy to offer her help or encouragement. I'd also like to thank Carrie Lavine, associate publisher, for her work; Dan Brodnitz and Damon Dean for their multimedia expertise; Alexa Riggs for coordinating production; Jan Haseman, Bob Bihlmayer, and Vicki Wilhite of London Road Design for, respectively, designing, desktop publishing, and proofreading the book; Cuong Le for creating the technical art; and Linda Facey for creating the index. Special thanks to Steve Lipson for introducing me to Sybex.

My thanks to Kevin Horst, Internet Assistant authority at Microsoft and technical editor extraordinaire, for making sure the manuscript was technically accurate. I'd also like to thank Brian Wilson, Microsoft's Internet Assistant product tester, for giving me his expert advice throughout the writing process.

Thanks to Ipswitch, Inc., for permission to use IFTP32 in my examples, and to Pixelsight, for permission to display their clip art.

I'd like to thank the wonderful staff of Direct Network Access (DNAI), the Internet service provider that hosts the Web Publishing Online Resource. Special thanks to President Dror Matalon for caring as much about people as he does about the Internet business.

Thanks to Sergé Wilson of the Berkeley Integration Group for putting together the sweetest hardware setup anyone could ask for.

The colorful logo for our fictitious business, Marvin's Magic Shoppe, is the result of a family collaboration: I thank my husband, Rael Dornfest, and my cousin, Hayley Weisner, for their inspired creativity.

I am grateful to Karen Einbinder for her treasured friendship (and for lending me her computer to write the original proposal for this book); to Joanne Miller for her advice and moral support; and to all of my friends who waited patiently (and bought me coffee) while I went into semi-seclusion to write this book.

I am indebted to my parents, Rosalyn and Jagdish Jirge, and Carol and Franklyn Dornfest, for their constant support and understanding.

Finally, I'd like to thank my wonderful husband, Rael Dornfest, who introduced me to the Internet in the first place. I owe so much of this book to his technical expertise, creativity, humor, and support. He inspires me to reach for new challenges every day.

TABLE OF CONTENTS

INTRODUCTION

You've been hearing about the Internet and the World Wide Web for some time now. All this talk of the information superhighway and global communication sounds pretty exciting, but it's all so *overwhelming*. How does a novice get to join in on all of the hubbub?

If you know how to use Microsoft Word for Windows 95, you can now explore the World Wide Web with the best of the computer experts. You can even create your own interactive documents and publish them for millions to see. *Do-It-Yourself Web Publishing with Word* will show you how to use Internet Assistant, a free add-on module for Word for Windows 95, to create and publish your own Web pages.

Unlike other manuals, you won't just sit on the couch and read about Internet Assistant, only to stare blankly at your computer when it comes time to get started. *Do-It-Yourself Web Publishing with Word* is a complete Web publishing tool kit. The CD included with this book contains Microsoft's Internet Assistant software, plus sample files to get you started on your home page. The examples take you through the entire process of creating a home page, step-by-step. Each step is fully illustrated, so that you can see what your screen should look like after each keystroke. When you are finished, you will have created a beautiful home page, complete with text, pictures, hyperlinks, interactive forms, and more.

You'll also be ready to explore the wide world of Web publishing even further. The *Web Publishing Online Resource,* located at **http://www.dnai.com/webpub**, is a constantly growing information source created especially for readers of this book. There, you'll find all the tools and tips you need to create state-of-the-art Web pages, plus all of the latest information about Internet Assistant. For more information, refer to "About the Web Publishing Online Resource" inside the back cover of the book.

This book is designed to be fun and easy to use, especially for a first-time user. No matter what your level of experience, this book will show you how to explore and contribute to the ever-growing realm of the World Wide Web.

Hardware and Software Requirements

Before you can get started with the examples in this book, you'll need the following computer equipment, software, and Internet connection:

- An IBM-compatible PC, with a 386DX or higher processor (486 recommended)
- 6 MB of memory (RAM), 8 MB recommended
- 4 MB of free hard disk space
- A VGA or higher-resolution monitor
- A CD-ROM drive
- A mouse or compatible pointing device
- A modem, preferably 14.4 BPS or higher
- Sound and video capability
- The Microsoft Windows 95 operating system (or Microsoft Windows NT Workstation operating system version 3.51 or later)
- English, French, German, or Italian language versions of Microsoft Word for Windows 95 (or Microsoft Word 6.0 for Windows NT)
- A full Internet connection
- Microsoft Internet Explorer Web browser (included with Microsoft Plus! or available for free download over the Internet)

 ► ► ► If you don't yet have an Internet connection, or if you have a connection but are not sure if it's the right type, refer to Appendix A, "Getting an Internet Connection," for details on how to find the best Internet service for you.

How This Book Is Organized

This book takes you through the process of creating a home page from start to finish. Each lesson builds upon what you have learned in the previous lesson, so you may find it helpful to start at the beginning and work through each chapter sequentially. However, if you'd rather pick and choose the steps you'd like to try, feel free to skip around.

 ▶ ▶ ▶ Throughout the book, I include notes that point out important details as we go along. Some notes also cross-reference related topics elsewhere in the book.

 ▶ ▶ ▶ I also provide tips on ways to make Web publishing with Internet Assistant even easier.

 ▶ ▶ ▶ Every now and then, I include warnings that alert you to potential trouble spots.

▶ ▶ ▶ **Sidebars**

I use sidebars to discuss interesting Web publishing and Internet-related topics in more detail.

Let's Get Started

You can begin with Lesson 1, "Getting Started," for a quick intro to the Internet and Web publishing, or you can skip ahead to Appendix B, "Installing Internet Assistant."

Let's go!

PART ONE

▽

GETTING ACQUAINTED
WITH INTERNET
ASSISTANT

1

GETTING STARTED

With all of the Internet jargon flying around in magazines, newspapers, and on TV, it's easy to wonder where to begin. Well, I'm here to tell you that you don't have to become a network expert to use Internet Assistant to browse and publish on the World Wide Web. This book will show you just how easy it is.

In this lesson, you'll find out what "Web publishing" means. You'll hear a little about how the Internet works and how the World Wide Web has made it easier to use than ever. You'll learn what it means to "create a home page." Finally, you'll launch Internet Assistant and become familiar with how it looks and what it can do.

The Internet: The Ultimate Soapbox

Publishing was once a mysterious process of conjuring up a topic, getting someone to pay you to put it on paper, writing the manuscript, editing it, writing and editing some more, designing the book, typesetting, proofreading, printing, distributing, and finally selling it in the form of a shiny new book. Only a chosen few were able to break into this field and have their works published for the world to see.

Now it's time to get those creative juices flowing, because the Internet has leveled the playing field. Today, anyone with a computer, an Internet connection, and a little know-how can be published before an unlimited audience.

You don't need to be a prize-winning journalist, graphics wizard, or big-time computer programmer to make yourself (or your company) known. You have the world's most powerful tool for distributing information right at your fingertips. This book will show you how to use it to publicize your business, to spread the word about a favorite cause, or simply to have some fun.

What Is the Internet?

A little background will help you understand what you are actually *doing* when you publish information on the Internet.

If you are already familiar with Internet basics, you can skip ahead to the section of this lesson called "Launching Internet Assistant."

The Internet is a global network of computers connected by telephone lines and high-speed links, as illustrated on the next page. When you use the Internet, you access information stored on these computers (called *servers*, since they serve you the information you want) by using your computer and modem to connect to an *Internet service provider* who, in turn, provides you with access to this vast network. An Internet service provider is a private company that has fast, powerful computers connected to the Internet via special, high-speed lines. It makes its livelihood by selling connect time and storage space to individuals and businesses who want to access and publish on the Internet.

The telephone system is a good analogy. Your telephone connects you to a widespread network of telephone lines all over the world. By pressing a specific set of numbers on your telephone keypad, you can reach just about anyone else who has a phone. Same with the Internet: your computer is like your phone, and you access different sites on the Internet by specifying their unique addresses (like dialing a phone number). Your Internet service provider is like the phone company, and the Internet is like the thousands of phone lines that crisscross the globe.

For more information about how to choose an Internet service provider, see Appendix A, "Getting an Internet Connection."

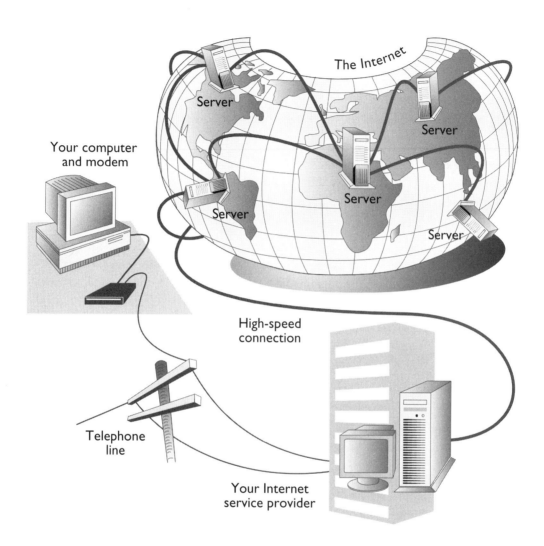

Your computer and modem

The Internet

Server

Server

Server

Server

Server

High-speed connection

Telephone line

Your Internet service provider

What Is the World Wide Web?

The World Wide Web (a.k.a. the Web, WWW, and W3) is only one of the features of the Internet (or the Net). While the two are not the same, the Web has become so popular that it is easy to see why people often think of it as the only way to get around the Net.

The Web has revolutionized the Internet by making it easy for the non-techie to navigate. In the same way that Windows makes the DOS interface more attractive and easier to use without changing its underlying structure, the Web puts a user-friendly mantle on top of the Internet's vast array of information. The Web isn't separate and distinct from the Internet, but, rather, it's an interface for exploring what is already there.

To view and navigate the Web, you need to use a special piece of software called a *Web browser*. Browsers (of which Internet Assistant is one) interpret the information stored on the Web, translate it into a readable form, and present you with the colorful documents you see on your screen. I'll go into detail about what Web browsers do in Lesson 2, "Browsing the Web."

The Web is made up of thousands of individual *websites*. A website is a particular place you can visit on the Web. Websites consist of one or more *Web pages* or *documents*. Like pages in a book, these pages are separate files that are all linked together to comprise the website as a whole.

When you hear people say they have a website or a *home page*, it means they have their own place on the Web to which you can direct your browser to find out more about them or their services. Their site may consist of a page (or more likely a bunch of interconnected pages) describing a product they offer, displaying their logo, and/or linking to other sites with related information.

 ▶ ▶ ▶ The term *home page* is often used to refer to three related (but different) things: a website as a whole, the opening or initial page of a website, and the "home base" page from which you begin each Web browsing session.

Here is a representation of a typical home page, not unlike the one you will create later on.

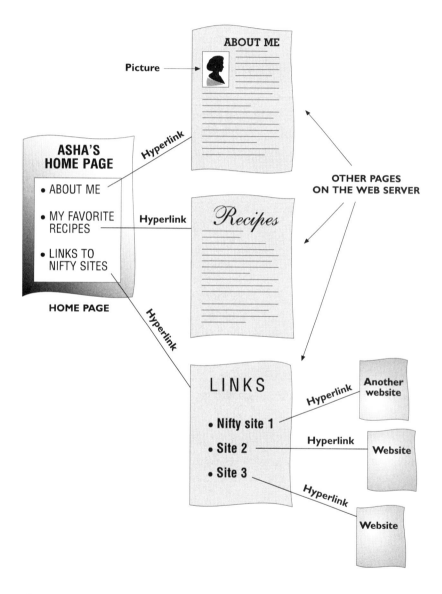

What are these links, you ask? The Web's star attraction is its use of *hyperlinks*. Hyperlinks connect Web documents and sites to one another, creating a seamless flow of information. A hyperlink is actually regular text that has been formatted to act as a springboard to another location. Clicking on the hyperlink transports you to another place in a Web page, another document on the same server, or another location on the Web altogether. You will find out just how powerful hyperlinks are in Lesson 2, "Browsing the Web."

In all of the Web's glamour and glory, the other fantastic features of the Internet tend to be overshadowed. I'll take a minute to mention the three most popular ones here: e-mail, FTP, and USENET newsgroups.

- Electronic mail, or *e-mail*, is perhaps the most widely used feature of the Internet. Using e-mail software, you can send messages to anyone else with an e-mail address. (When you see a notation that looks something like **name@organization.com**, it's an e-mail address.)
- File Transfer Protocol, or *FTP*, gives you access to the gigabytes of free software available on the Internet. You use an FTP program to log on to a public-access computer (called an *anonymous FTP site*) and download software from that computer to yours.
- *USENET newsgroups* are some of the more dynamic places to visit on the Internet. A newsgroup is like an electronic discussion group; it is devoted to a particular topic, and anyone can join in, post their opinions, and respond to other people's posts. There's a newsgroup for just about every topic you can think of, plus a few that you probably would never dream of in a million years. Newsreader software lets you select the newsgroups to which you'd like to subscribe (read on an ongoing basis), and then displays the day's posts for you to read at will. Be careful... newsgroups can be addictive!

The programs I've mentioned above are usually included by your Internet service provider in the software package you get when you sign up for an account. There are also commercially available packages, but why pay for software you can (and should) get for free?

► ► ► The Web Publishing Online Resource includes links to lots of popular Internet shareware, including e-mail programs, newsreaders, FTP programs, and more. Feel free to download a few and try them out. You'll find the Online Resource at **http://www.dnai.com/webpub**. If you're not sure how to access this website, the next lesson, "Browsing the Web," will show you how.

What Is Web Publishing?

We've talked about how easy it is to browse the Web, but the exciting news is how easy it is to put your *own* home page on the Web for others to see. This is called *Web publishing*, and it is Internet Assistant's main reason for being.

When you publish information on the Web, you do two things: you create one or several Web pages, and you make them publicly accessible on the Web.

A Web page is just like any other computer file (say a word processing document or a spreadsheet), except that it is written using a special language called *Hypertext Markup Language*, or *HTML*. HTML is nothing more than a set of plain text codes that define the structure of the page. Your Web browser then interprets those codes (called *tags*) and presents you with the nicely formatted documents you see while surfing the Web. The illustration below gives you a before-and-after look at a page of HTML *au naturel* on the left, and, on the right, how it looks as seen through a Web browser.

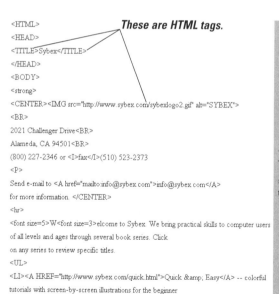

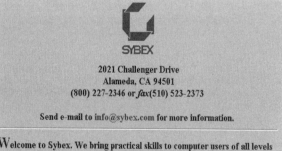

Internet Assistant saves you from having to learn all of HTML's different tags. It is an *HTML editor*, a special program that inserts HTML tags for you. The kicker is that you get to use the familiar interface of Microsoft Word, and Internet Assistant does the HTML dirty work.

▶ ▶ ▶ **Y**ou'll try your hand at Web publishing and get your first look at real HTML tags in Lesson 3, "Creating Your Home Page." You'll make your pages accessible on the Web in Lesson 11, "Putting Your Home Page on the Web."

Launching Internet Assistant

Now that you have some background on the Internet and Web publishing, let's take a look at Internet Assistant.

  ▶ ▶ ▶ **I**f you haven't already, now is the time to install Internet Assistant on your computer. Appendix B, "Installing Internet Assistant," contains simple instructions for accomplishing this using the CD that comes with this book.

"Launching" may seem a misleading term, since, after it's installed, Internet Assistant exists *within* Word and is automatically available each time you open Word. You'll notice that Word looks and acts almost exactly as it did before you installed Internet Assistant; maybe there are a couple of new buttons and menu items here and there, but little else has changed.

Or has it?

Your humble word processor now can do more than just crank out memos and letters—with Internet Assistant you can use Word to explore and publish on the Web. Internet Assistant has transformed Word into both a Web browser and an HTML editor.

Let's take a look at what is different about Word now that it includes Internet Assistant.

1 Open Word by clicking on the **Start** button and selecting **Microsoft Word**.

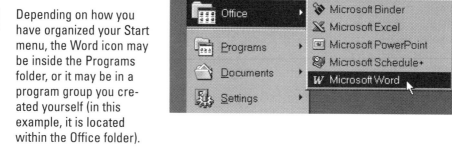

▶ Depending on how you have organized your Start menu, the Word icon may be inside the Programs folder, or it may be in a program group you created yourself (in this example, it is located within the Office folder).

▶ Word opens and presents you with a blank document. The screen doesn't look much different than it did before you installed Internet Assistant, does it?

2 From the Word menu bar, select **View ➤ Toolbars**.

▶ The Toolbars dialog box appears. A toolbar is a row of buttons and fields that appears underneath the Word menu bar on your screen. You can use toolbars to speed up tasks you tend to do often while creating a document. This dialog box allows you to choose which toolbars you would like to display.

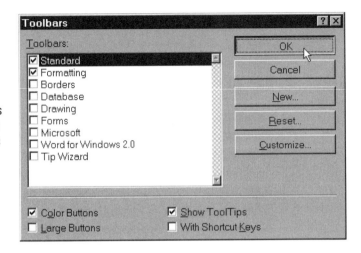

3 If they're not already checked, mark the **Standard** and **Formatting** checkboxes.

4 Click on the **OK** button.

▶ The Standard and Formatting toolbars appear. They contain some of the most frequently used editing and formatting tools.

▶ The Formatting toolbar also contains evidence of Internet Assistant's presence: the Switch to Web Browse View button.

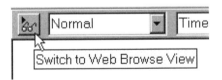

By resetting the toolbar option in Word's default document template (Normal.dot) to include the Standard and Formatting toolbars, you tell Word to automatically display those toolbars each time it opens. To do this, select View ➤ Toolbars, make sure the Standard and Formatting checkboxes are marked, and click on the Reset button. Then, click on the OK button when prompted.

Now let's see what that little button can do.

Switching between Web Browse and HTML Edit Views

As I mentioned earlier, a browser is a program that lets you navigate the Web, and an HTML editor is a program you use to create Web pages. Internet Assistant combines both functions into one package. Depending upon which function you would like to use, you can easily switch between *Web Browse view* and *HTML Edit view*.

When I refer here to "views," I am talking about the way in which Internet Assistant's capabilities are differentiated. Web browsing and HTML editing are two very different tasks that usually require two very different pieces of software. Internet Assistant deals with this by giving you a convenient little button which allows you to alternate between these two modes.

While in Web Browse view, you can look at pages on the Web. You cannot, however, create or modify any type of document. To do this, you must switch to HTML Edit view, which allows you to create and make changes to HTML and regular Word documents on your computer.

Let's see exactly what we're talking about here.

1 Click on the **Switch to Web Browse View** button.

Click here.

▶ Notice how the toolbar and menu bar items change. Word suddenly looks just like a Web browser, which is exactly what it has become. While you are in Web Browse view, you can use Word to look at and navigate around the Web (in the next lesson, we'll take the browser for a spin).

▶ Also, notice how the Switch to Web Browse View button has changed faces: it has become the Switch to Edit View button.

2 Click on the **Switch to Edit View** button.

▶ The original menu bar and toolbars reappear. This is Word's default view, since, in this view, you can create new documents and make changes to existing ones.

▶ ▶ ▶ **I**nternet Assistant includes an excellent built-in Help system. It's a great reference, and you can access it whenever you are using Internet Assistant to browse the Web and/or create Web documents. To get help, select Help ➤ Internet Assistant for Word Help.

Now that you've taken a quick glimpse at Internet Assistant, let's exit the program.

Exiting Internet Assistant

You guessed it…exiting Internet Assistant is the same as exiting Word, since it lives within Word's structure.

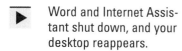 Select **File** ➣ **Exit.**

Word and Internet Assistant shut down, and your desktop reappears.

You now have some background on the Internet, the Web, and Web publishing. You've also been introduced to Word's new, turbo-charged capabilities as a Web browser and an HTML editor. If you're ready for some adventure, read on! In Lesson 2, you'll make the leap from your desktop into cyberspace using Internet Assistant as your vehicle.

BROWSING THE WEB

In Lesson 1, I talked about how easy it is to explore (or in Net-lingo, *surf*) the Web. Its ease of use is only part of the reason everyone is so enamored with the Web. In addition to letting you jump from place to place with the click of your mouse, the Web presents you with dazzling images and multimedia effects. The Internet never looked this good!

In this lesson, we'll get to know Internet Assistant's browsing features. We'll use Internet Assistant to look at pages that are already stored on your computer and also to view pages on the Web.

▶ ▶ ▶ **I**f you already know how to use a Web browser, or if you're itching to get started on your home page, you can jump to Lesson 3, "Creating Your Home Page."

Viewing Pages Located on Your Computer

As a part of the setup process, Internet Assistant installed a number of document files onto your computer's hard drive. These documents contain lots of information about getting up and running with Internet Assistant. Viewing them will give you a good introduction to Internet Assistant, as well as familiarize you with the way Web pages look and act. Because these pages are *local* (they are stored on your computer's hard drive rather than on a Web server), you don't need to be connected to the Internet to be able to look at them.

▶ ▶ ▶

All Hyperlinks Are Not Created Equal

While the pages that come with Internet Assistant may look and act like Web pages, they are *not* the same. They are actually regular Word documents with pictures and links inserted into the text. Real Web pages are written in HTML, are stored on an Internet service provider's Web server, and can be read by any computer with an Internet connection and a Web browser. These documents, on the other hand, can't be viewed using another Web browser, and will only work on a computer with Word 95 and Internet Assistant installed on its system. The easiest way to tell what type of document you're working with is to notice the *file name extension,* the three-letter code that follows the name of the file. All formatted Word documents have the extension .doc, while HTML files have the extension .htm (if they are created on a non-Windows platform such as Macintosh or UNIX, they have the extension .html).

1 Open Word by clicking on the **Start** button and selecting **Microsoft Word.**

▶ Word opens and presents you with a blank document.

2 Select **File** ➢ **Browse Web.**

▶ Internet Assistant's home page, *default.doc*, appears. It is called a "home page" in this case because it is your default starting point each time you begin a browsing session. Why did you select Browse Web rather than simply clicking the Switch to Web Browse View button? Because selecting Browse Web tells Word to open *default.doc* as well as switch you into Web Browse view. Clicking the Switch to Web Browse View button switches views, but does not load Internet Assistant's home page.

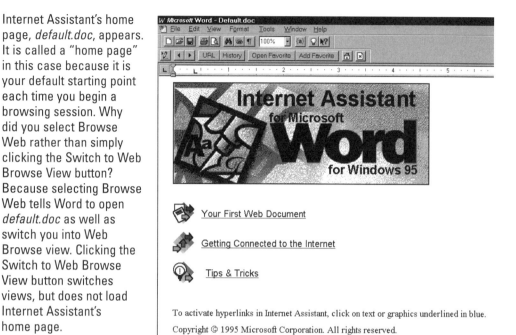

Click on any text that is blue and underlined.

3 Click on any of the blue, underlined words or phrases you see.

Your First Web Document

Getting Connected to the Internet

Tips & Tricks

▶ You jump to another one of Internet Assistant's local documents.

The big news is that you have just activated a hyperlink! I mentioned earlier that hyperlinks are the method of travel on the Web, and as you can see, they instantly transport you to a different location within a page, or to a different page altogether. Whenever you see highlighted, underlined text in a Web page (or in this case, a Word document), you can click on that text to jump somewhere else. The default color for hyperlinks is blue, but many pages on the Web use other colors.

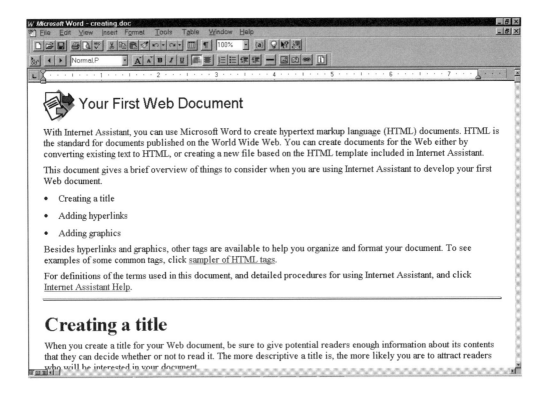

4 Click on any other hyperlinks in the page to see how they work.

5 When you're ready to move on, click on the **Home** button in the toolbar (or select **Window ➤ Home**) to return to Internet Assistant's home page.

Internet Assistant's
home page reappears.

 Internet Assistant: Microsoft Word with Multiple Personalities

Unlike a regular Web browser, which simply accesses information on the Web and displays it on your screen, Internet Assistant actually opens the documents you browse (click on the Window menu and notice how all of the documents you just viewed are currently open). Remember, Internet Assistant is a word processor at its core. The only way it can approximate the experience of Web browsing is to open the documents you request and display them using a Word template that interprets HTML tags. Internet Assistant uses a template called *webview.dot* to display HTML documents in their "browsable" forms.

Exploring the Web with Internet Assistant

Now that you've experimented with hyperlinks on local pages, you are ready to look at HTML documents in their natural habitat, the World Wide Web. Fasten your seat belts, because you're about to leave the cozy comfort of your hard drive and enter the exciting realm of cyberspace.

If the pages look a bit different than in the examples, don't worry. The point of our tour is to familiarize you with Internet Assistant's browsing features. The beauty of the Web is that it changes all the time as Web publishers add information and goodies to their websites. Enjoy!

  If you're not logged on to the Internet, you should activate your connection now. If you don't know how to activate your connection, contact your Internet service provider's customer support staff. If you don't have an Internet connection, refer to Appendix A, "Getting an Internet Connection," for tips on how to choose an Internet service provider.

You can start exploring the Web at the website of your choice. All you need to know is where to begin. A *universal resource locator*, or *URL*, is the technical name for a website address. For example, the URL for Sybex's website is **http://www.sybex.com**. This cryptic-looking bunch of letters, dots, and slashes tells your Web browser where to go to find the page you want, which page to retrieve, and how to retrieve it. Every single page on the Web has its own URL, and each one follows these conventions:

- It begins with **http://**. An abbreviation for *hypertext transfer protocol,* this code identifies the address to your browser as a World Wide Web URL. URLs for other types of servers are identified differently. For example, URLs for FTP servers begin with **ftp://**.
- Next comes the name of the Web server upon which the site resides (for example, **www.sybex.com**). **www** refers to the name of the Web server itself. **sybex.com** is the *domain name*, which means that Sybex maintains this particular server. The **.com** at the end indicates that this is a commercial site. Other types of sites include educational (**http://www.berkeley.edu**), government (**http://www.whitehouse.gov**), and nonprofit organizations (**http: //www.npr.org**). While this is the standard URL formatting scheme, it isn't mandatory. Don't be surprised if you see a URL that looks a little different.

This is all some Web URLs need to be complete. Sometimes, however, URLs include additional slashes and names. This information points to specific directories and files on the Web server. For example, the URL **http://www.sybex.com/internet.html** will bypass Sybex's home page and take you directly to the page that describes Sybex's Internet books (**internet.html**).

Which brings up an important point: if you know its URL, you can go directly to *any* page on the Web. You don't need to go to the home page of its site first.

 ▶ ▶ ▶ **I**nternet Assistant has a convenient feature called *automatic protocol detection* which means that you don't have to type the **http://** (or **ftp://**, etc.) part of the URL to go to a particular site. For example, if you want to visit the Web Publishing Online Resource, you need only type **www. dnai.com/webpub**. Not all browsers have automatic protocol detection, however, which is why the **http://** is generally included when mentioning a URL.

Are you feeling comfortable with URLs? Good. Now let's go websurfing. The first stop on our web tour is Yahoo, an Internet index.

1 While in Web Browse view, click on the **URL** button in the toolbar (or select **File ➢ Open URL**).

▶ The Open URL dialog box appears. Here, you specify the URL of the site you would like to visit.

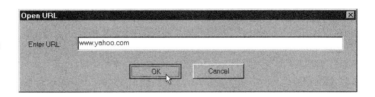

2 In the Enter URL field, type **www.yahoo.com**.

3 Click on the **OK** button.

These "buttons" are hyperlinks within the graphic.

Yahoo is Hiring · Reuters News Stories · Web Launch

Search Options

▶ A status bar appears indicating that Internet Assistant is downloading the page. It takes a few moments for the pictures that are part of Yahoo's home page to appear. This is because the images are actually distinct files that are retrieved separately from the text of the document. Small images take a few seconds to load. Larger images can take much longer. Once the graphics load, the Yahoo home page appears.

- **Arts** - - *Literature*, *Photography*, *Architecture*, *...*

- **Business and Economy [Xtra!]** - - *Directory*, *Investments*, *Classifieds*, *...*

- **Computers and Internet** - - *Internet*, *WWW*, *Software*, *Multimedia*, *...*

- **Education** - - *Universities*, *K-12*, *Courses*, *...*

- **Entertainment [Xtra!]** - - *TV*, *Movies*, *Music*, *Magazines*, *Books*, *...*

- **Government** - - *Politics* *[Xtra!]*, *Agencies*, *Law*, *Military*, *...*

Text hyperlinks

This is a popular stop for many Web explorers who are looking for a particular piece of information. Yahoo is a *Web index*—an overview of the Web arranged by subject (see the sidebar entitled "Is It on the Web?" a little later in the chapter for more information about Web indices). Yahoo is a great place to start websurfing when you want to see what's out there.

To look around the website, you can click on one of the text hyperlinks (the words and phrases that are underlined and blue) or you can click on a *graphic hyperlink*. A graphic hyperlink works just like a text hyperlink, except you click on pictures that are outlined in blue to move to another place in the website. Feel free to look around—click on any of the hyperlinks that interest you. You will jump to other pages in the website that contain more hyperlinks to yet other locations within the site, or to one of the thousands of websites indexed there. Keep exploring to your heart's content (that's what the Web is all about!).

Notice Yahoo's colorful opening graphic. It does more than just add personality—this is a good example of a special kind of graphic hyperlink called an *imagemap* or *ISMAP graphic*. The picture itself contains several hyperlinks to different locations; you click on the "buttons" inside the graphic to go to other pages in the Yahoo website. Pictures that double as hyperlinks are surrounded by a blue border, so you know whether or not you can click on them to jump somewhere else.

After a while, websurfing can leave you feeling like you are wandering in a dense forest of information. Don't worry—Internet Assistant leaves a trail of breadcrumbs for you to follow back home. If you would like to move back to a previous page, click on the Go Back button. You'll go back, in order, through the pages you have visited so far. To return to your present location from a previous page, click on the Go Forward button. (You can also use the menu bar to navigate: select Window ➢ Go Back or Window ➢ Go Forward.)

Go Back   Go Forward

▶ ▶ ▶ **S**ome websites take a long time to load (they may contain large, complex graphics, for example). If, while you're browsing, you wish to stop a page while it's downloading, you can click on the Cancel button in the Downloading File dialog box or the Stop button in the toolbar (the one that has a picture of a page with a little red *x* on it) to stop the download process. If you stopped the downloading process after the new page has begun to appear on your screen, you can click on the Go Back button to view the previous page you visited, or you can select File ➤ Reload to download the page again and view it in its entirety.

In addition to browsing the contents of Yahoo, you can also search for a particular topic. How? By using one of HTML's more brilliant features, an *interactive form*. An interactive form is like a paper form in that it contains *fields* you can fill out. It allows you to interact with the website by submitting the information you fill in the form. Yahoo uses a form to collect the information it needs to perform a search for a topic or a keyword. Let's watch an interactive form in action: let's do a search.

1 If you have already followed a few of Yahoo's links, click on the **Go Back** button to return to Yahoo's home page.

▶ Yahoo's home page appears. Toward the top of the screen is an empty box and, next to it, a button that says *Search*. The box is the *field* where you can type a word for which you would like Yahoo to search. This is the simplest example of a form—it contains only one field and one button.

2 Click on the field and type the word **elvis.**

▶ *elvis* appears in the field.

3 Click on the **Search** button.

▶ The information you entered is submitted to Yahoo's server, which performs a search of its contents. Once it's finished, a page full of links to all the references that mention *elvis* appears.

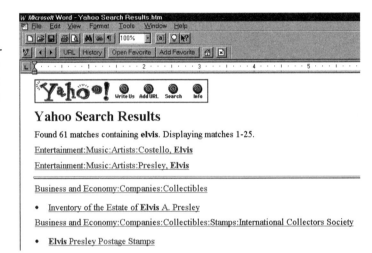

Pretty impressive, isn't it? Just think how handy this will be once you start using the Web as a research tool.

Is It on the Web?

Now that you are a true websurfer, you'll find yourself asking this question all the time. Whenever you need to do some research on a company, find an obscure little fact, or figure out what to make for dinner, chances are you'll turn to the Web for answers. As you've probably noticed, however, the Web is a big place, and the information you want is not necessarily at your fingertips—you have to dig for it. Luckily, there are several fantastic search utilities and indices on the Web (of which Yahoo is but one). When you use these, you'll usually find the information you want in just a few clicks.

(continued)

I've included links to the Web's most popular search tools in the Online Resource at **http://www.dnai.com/webpub**.

Making Browsing Even Easier

Internet Assistant contains several handy features that allow you to customize and organize your Web browsing sessions.

Using Your History List

If you want to return to a page you recently visited, but you don't want to click on the Go Back button a million times, you can use your *History List* to transport yourself directly there. Your History List contains the titles and URLs of the last 50 sites you visited. Let's use your History List to return to Yahoo's home page.

1 Click on the **History** button in the Web Browse View toolbar (or select **Window** ➤ **History List**).

▶ The History List appears.

2 Double-click on **Yahoo.**

▶ You jump directly to Yahoo's home page.

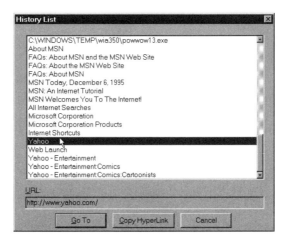

See how easy it can be to get around?

Adding Links to Your Favorite Places List

You'll probably find yourself visiting Yahoo again and again as you search for tidbits of information. For this reason, you may wish to add it to your Favorite Places list. Your Favorite Places list is a local page on which you can store hyperlinks to all of the websites you want to visit again another time. Internet Assistant makes it easy to add links while you are browsing. After that, all you have to do is open your Favorite Places list whenever you want a direct link to your favorite websites.

Let's add a link to Yahoo on your Favorite Places list.

1   With Yahoo's home page visible, click on the **Add Favorite** button in the toolbar (or select **Tools ➤ Add to Favorite Places**).

▶   Internet Assistant automatically inserts a link to Yahoo on your Favorite Places list.

2   To view your Favorite Places list, click on the **Open Favorite** button in the toolbar (or select **Tools ➤ Open Favorite**).

▶   Your Favorite Places list appears, and, as you can see, it contains a hyperlink to Yahoo.

 Favorite Places

Any time you view a document you'd like to add to this list, you can easily do so by choosing the Add Favorite button on the toolbar. To delete an item from the list, switch to Edit view, select the item, and choose DELETE.

Microsoft Network Home Page: A great place to start exploring the Internet

Yahoo

Now you'll never have to remember Yahoo's URL again...just click on the hyperlink stored on your Favorite Places list, and you're there.

  ► ► ► **T**o remove an entry or add your own text to the Favorite Places list, click on the Switch to HTML Edit button. While in HTML Edit view, you can make any changes you like to the page. When you are through, select File ≻ Save to save your changes.

Turning Off Image Loading

When you want to quickly gather information on the Web, you won't want to wait while Internet Assistant loads the graphics on every site you visit. For this reason, you can choose to turn off *image loading* while you browse. With image loading turned off, Internet Assistant skips the graphics files and just loads the site's text. A bit utilitarian, perhaps, but very handy when you want fast information.

Let's try it now.

1 Return to the Yahoo home page by clicking on the **Go Back** button or by using your History List.

2 Select **View** ≻ **Load Images [on]**. This menu item *toggles* image loading on and off. Toggling is like flipping a switch, and the current setting is displayed by [on]. By selecting it, you are switching the setting to [off].

3 Select **File** ➢ **Reload** to view Yahoo without its graphics.

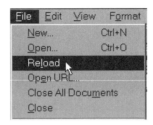

▶ Internet Assistant reloads Yahoo's home page, this time without the graphics (a little blue square has replaced them).

4 To view the site's graphics again, select **View** ➢ **Load Images [off]** (which toggles the setting back to [on]).

5 Select **File** ➢ **Reload** to retrieve the page again, this time with all of the pictures.

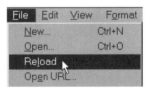

▶ The Yahoo home page reappears with graphics intact.

Ending Your Browsing Session

Let's put our web-surfboard away for now and end our browsing session.

1   Select **File** ➢ **Close All Documents.** (Or, if you feel like taking a break, select File ➢ Exit.)

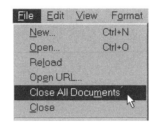

▶   A Microsoft Word dialog box appears, asking if you want to save changes to Yahoo.htm. When you typed information into Yahoo's search form (remember *elvis*?), Internet Assistant reacted as if you were making a change to a regular Word document.

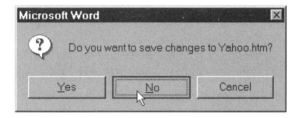

2   Click on the **No** button.

▶   Word closes all of the Web documents you have visited and leaves you with an empty document window, or if you chose to exit, your desktop reappears.

If you had clicked on the Yes button when asked if you wanted to save Yahoo.htm, Internet Assistant would have saved a *copy* of Yahoo's home page file on your hard drive. It would not affect the original Yahoo home page, which is safely tucked away on its own Web server (only Yahoo's system administrators can make changes to its home page). As for the copy on your hard drive, it would be useless, because all of its links are *relative*, which means that they are dependent upon the location of the Web page. The links only work on Yahoo's Web server, not your hard drive. We'll talk more about *relative hyperlinks* in Lesson 5, "Creating Hyperlinks."

We have reached the end of our Web adventure for now, but for you it is only the beginning. There are endless links to follow to fascinating sites all over the world, and the Online Resource is a great place to start. Have fun!

Exploring the Web Using Other Browsers

Throughout this lesson I've talked about how Internet Assistant isn't a "real" Web browser; it's actually a word processor in browser's clothing. Now that you've had a chance to try it out, you can compare it with other Web browsers.

While Internet Assistant is a great tool for Web publishing (as you will soon learn), its capabilities as a browser are limited. Why? Because it is, at its core, a word processor. Internet Assistant is a natural when it comes to writing HTML documents because it takes advantage of Word's elegant interface. As a browser, however, it is more clumsy.

Internet Assistant's browser doesn't recognize some of the newest and spiffiest features of HTML, including colorful Web page formatting and layout effects. It also doesn't support integrated capabilities such as sending e-mail messages directly from a Web page (to name only one). When you use Internet Assistant's browser, you are missing out on some of the most exciting effects the Web has to offer.

For this reason, I recommend that if you intend to do any serious websurfing (and believe me, you will!), use a full-fledged Web browser. Not only will your ride on the Web be smoother and faster, you will be able to enjoy all of its goodies and features.

The dueling leaders in the war of the Web browsers are Netscape Navigator and Microsoft's Internet Explorer. One of the reasons Web publishers prefer these two browsers is because they make use of *browser-specific extensions to HTML.* What this means is that each company has created special HTML tags that produce amazing design effects—when viewed through *their* browser. The good news is that Web publishers have more ways to enhance their Web pages with interesting design effects. The bad news is that those effects are only visible to readers who are using the appropriate browser.

Netscape is a sophisticated browser that supports many of the Web's latest developments. You can read about all of Netscape's amazing features, and how to take advantage of them while Web publishing, in Sybex's book *Surfing the Internet with Netscape* by Daniel A. Tauber and Brenda Kienan.

Internet Explorer is an equally powerful browser with its own advantages. It supports several impressive HTML design effects of its own and has the added plus of fitting nicely into your Windows 95 interface. What's more, Internet Assistant includes built-in support for several of Explorer's fancy effects, making it easy to create sophisticated Web pages for those of your readers who use the Explorer browser.

You're probably bracing yourself for how much these sophisticated pieces of software will set you back. Well, relax, because both Internet Explorer and Netscape (and many other browsers) are free for evaluation and available for you to download to your computer from the Internet.

Visit the Online Resource (**http://www.dnai.com/webpub**), where you'll find links to the home pages of several of the most popular Web browsers. Download one or two using an FTP program and take them for a test surf to see which one you like best. One of your choices should be Internet Explorer, because I use it to demonstrate several of Internet Assistant's features later in the book. You will be amazed when you see the Web's true colors.

Okay, enough about browsing! In the next lesson, you'll move on to creating your own home page.

PART TWO

PUBLISHING BASICS

3

CREATING YOUR HOME PAGE

Now that you've had a chance to see what's out there, you're ready to start creating a page of your own. Imagine...your website will be on a par with the big guys when it comes to having a voice on the Web. Here is your chance to tell the world about your company, your cause, or yourself!

In Lesson 2, you got to know Internet Assistant's browsing features. In this lesson, you'll start using its HTML editing features to build a site for an imaginary business, Marvin's Magic Shoppe. You'll take the beginning steps of creating a new HTML document, titling it, and saving it. You'll then take your first look at the HTML tags themselves.

Creating a New HTML Document

Here is where you will begin to see Internet Assistant's genius, because it makes HTML editing just about as easy as word processing. Let's create the first page of your site, the home page. (Later on, you will create more pages, and you'll link them to this one).

1   Open Word by clicking on the **Start** button and selecting **Microsoft Word.**

▶   Word opens and presents you with a blank document.

2 Select **File** ➤ **New**.

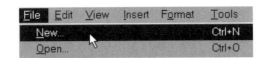

▶ The New dialog box appears. Here, you can choose what type of new document you would like to create. Word will open a new document based upon the template you select. In this case, you will create a new HTML document (which is based upon the *html.dot* template).

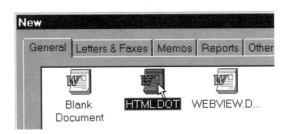

3 Double-click on **HTML.DOT**.

▶ A new document opens. It looks very similar to the Word document that opened earlier; however, notice how the Standard and Formatting toolbars have changed. New tools have appeared, showing that you are now in HTML Edit view and that you are working on an HTML document (we'll go through each of these tools in detail as we go along).

HTML editing tools

▶ ▶ ▶ To create a new HTML document, you must select File ➤ New to display the New dialog box. If you click on the New button in the toolbar, or if you use the keyboard shortcut Ctrl+N, Word will bypass the dialog box and create a regular Word file.

Now that you have created a new HTML document, let's add the text. Since this will be your home page, its main purpose is to act as a table of contents for the rest of your site.

1 It is always good to put a heading at the top of your page that clearly identifies what it's about. Type **Marvin's Magic Shoppe** and press the **Return** key (↵).

Marvin's Magic Shoppe

2 A welcome message is a nice way to greet visitors to your site. Type **Welcome to Marvin's! Marvin is proud to be your guide through the dazzling world of magic.** ↵.

Marvin's Magic Shoppe

Welcome to Marvin's! Marvin is proud to be your guide through the dazzling world of magic.

3 Type **About Marvin's** ↵ **Catalog of Wares** ↵ **Tell Marvin What You Think.** This is the important part of the page: the list of the site's contents. In Lesson 5, you'll hyperlink the items in this list to other pages that contain more detail.

magic.

About Marvin's

Catalog of Wares

Tell Marvin What You Think

Adding a Title

Adding a title to your Web page seems a tiny detail. After all, it says "Marvin's Magic Shoppe" at the top of the page, right? While that's true, a title is different than a heading. The title describes your document to other Web browsers without appearing in the text of the document itself.

Where the URL is the *address* of a Web document, the title is its *name*. The title appears in the title bar at the top of your Web browser's viewing window when you visit a page. It is what is displayed when you add a website to your Favorite Places list. It is also the name that appears in your History List. Titling each of your Web pages is an easy detail to forget, but it's one of the touches that makes your page look finished and professional.

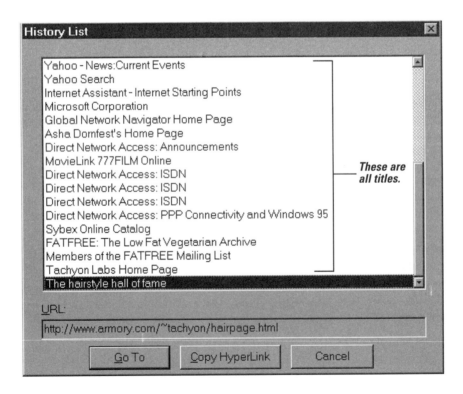

Let's add a title to your home page.

1 In the Formatting toolbar, click on the **Title** button (or select **File ➢ HTML Document Info**).

▶ The HTML Document Head Information dialog box appears. This is where you specify the title of your document.

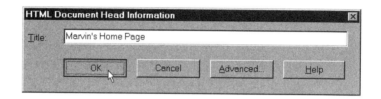

2 Type **Marvin's Home Page**.

3 Click on the **OK** button.

▶ While nothing appears to have changed, your Web page now has the title *Marvin's Home Page*.

 ▶ ▶ ▶ **U**nless you title *each* of your Web pages (not just the home page), Internet Assistant will substitute "HTML Document for the World Wide Web" as its title.

Saving an HTML Document

By now this is a familiar refrain—saving an HTML document using Internet Assistant is just like saving a regular Word document.

1 Select **File ➢ Save**.

▶ The Save As dialog box appears.

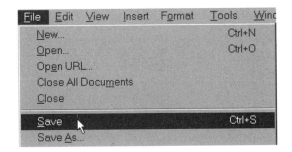

There are a few things to notice here. First, Word has automatically filled in a file name by using the first word of your document (we'll change the file name in a moment, but it's a nifty feature). Second, notice the file name extension: .htm. As I mentioned earlier, the .htm extension identifies this document as an HTML document. Finally, take note of the *destination folder* (the folder in which you are saving your file). Throughout the book, we'll use Word's default destination folder, called My Documents, to store your HTML documents while you are working on them.

2 In the File name field, type **home** (you don't need to type .htm—Word will do it for you). *Home* is a logical file name for your home page while you are in the process of creating a site. As a general rule, short and understandable file names are always best.

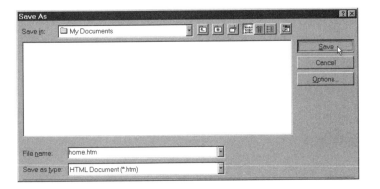

3 Click on the **Save** button.

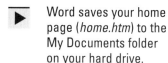

Word saves your home page (*home.htm*) to the My Documents folder on your hard drive.

> **Converting a Regular Word Document to HTML**
>
> You don't always need to start from scratch; you may already have well-organized informational and/or promotional literature that you would simply like to convert into a Web page.
>
> One of Internet Assistant's most useful features is the ease with which you can take a Word document (formatted or not) and turn it into a page suitable for publishing on the Web. Simply open any Word document and select File ➤ Save As. The Save As dialog box appears. In the Save as type: field, select HTML document (.htm), and click on the OK button. Internet Assistant will convert the document to HTML format and will save it on your hard drive. Once the document is converted, you can add HTML formatting effects to enhance the look of the page (Lesson 4 shows you how). For more information on converting Word documents to HTML—including what *can't* be converted—refer to the Internet Assistant Help system.

Viewing HTML Tags

Until now, creating an HTML page hasn't looked or seemed much different than creating a Word document. That's because Internet Assistant has quietly been doing the HTML work behind the scenes. Now you will see exactly what it has been doing. You will view the "bones" of your HTML page: the *HTML tags* themselves. HTML tags are the formatting and structure codes that identify your document to the rest of the Web as an HTML document, and define what it will look like when viewed through a Web browser. Internet Assistant keeps these tags hidden while you work so that your page appears nice and clutter-free, but in reality, it is filled with codes that are scattered throughout the page.

Let's take a look at the HTML tags, which in Internet Assistant lingo is called *viewing HTML source*.

1 Select **View** ➤
HTML Source.

▶ Your page appears with all of its HTML tags showing. The HTML tags are the bits of text that appear inside the angle brackets (**<HTML>** and **<TITLE>**, for example). Most of the tags you see here were inserted automatically by Internet Assistant, but some were added because of the text you typed (believe it or not!). Remember the invisible title you added to your page? Here it is, hidden inside the HTML source. Each time you typed a ↵, Internet Assistant inserted the HTML tag **<P>** (for paragraph).

<HTML>

<HEAD>

<TITLE>Marvin's Home Page</TITLE>

<META NAME="GENERATOR" CONTENT="Internet Assistant for Microsoft Word 2.0z">
</HEAD>

<BODY>

<P>
Marvin's Magic Shoppe
<P>
Welcome to Marvin's! Marvin is proud to be your guide through the dazzling world of magic.

▶ Also, a tiny HTML window appears on your screen. This window contains two buttons: the Auto Format HTML button and the Return to Edit Mode button. The Auto Format HTML button color-codes your HTML source so that you can easily distinguish between the HTML tags and the text that you've entered. The Return to Edit Mode button is your escape hatch back to the neat, tidy, non-HTML world.

2 Click on the **Auto Format HTML** button.

▶ There is a momentary pause as Internet Assistant automatically formats your document, then the Microsoft Word dialog box appears telling you that the auto format was completed successfully.

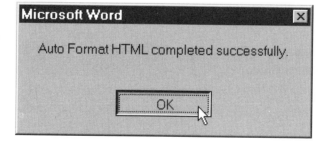

3 Click on the **OK** button.

▶ The HTML source is now color coded, making HTML tags and text stand apart from each other. This feature comes in very handy if you like to edit your document directly at the source (we'll talk about how to edit HTML source in Lesson 9).

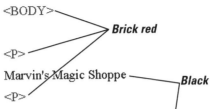

<BODY>

Brick red

<P>

Marvin's Magic Shoppe — *Black*

<P>

Welcome to Marvin's! Marvin is proud to be your guide through the dazzling world of magic.

4 Click on the **Return to Edit Mode** button.

▶ The HTML tags disappear, and you return to regular HTML Edit view. From here, let's close up shop for this lesson.

5 Select **File** ➤ **Exit** (or, if you want to continue with the next lesson, select File ➤ Close).

▶ Your desktop appears (or, if you decided not to exit Word, an empty document window appears).

▶ ▶ ▶ If, while viewing HTML Source, you click on the little button with the *x* on it in the HTML window (making it disappear), fear not—you can still return to regular HTML Edit view. Select View ➤ Toolbars, mark the check box next to the HTML option, and click on the OK button. The toolbar will reappear, and you can then click on the Return to Edit Mode button.

Viewing HTML source may look like a bunch of gobbledygook right now, but as you develop your Web publishing skills, it will become a useful tool. You can view the HTML source of any page on the Web, which means that you can peek at the structure of pages you particularly like. When I'm websurfing and I come across a page that makes me wonder "How did they do that?" I view HTML source and find out.

  ▶ ▶ ▶ Internet Assistant's Help system contains a chart of HTML tags and their Word equivalents. This is a handy reference when you see an HTML tag in a Web document and you want to know how to use it with Internet Assistant's commands. To see this chart, select Help ➤ Internet Assistant for Word Help from the Internet Assistant menu bar. The Help dialog box will appear. With the Contents tab active, double-click on HTML/Word Equivalents. A list of contents will appear. Double-click on HTML Tags and Equivalent Word Commands.

In this lesson, you've dipped your pinkie toe into the world of Web publishing: you've created a new HTML document and started work on your home page, and you've viewed HTML source. You are now ready to use HTML formatting effects to make your page (along with the other HTML documents contained on the CD) look more attractive. In Lesson 4, you'll use Internet Assistant to enhance your pages with text styles, lists, and much more.

ENHANCING YOUR WEB PAGES WITH FORMATTING

In Lesson 3, you created the basis for your website: the home page. Now it's time to brighten it up! In this lesson, you'll learn how to use Internet Assistant's HTML formatting options to add visual interest to your pages.

All HTML documents start out as plain vanilla text, with no variation whatsoever (case in point: the home page you just created). Internet Assistant formats your documents by inserting HTML tags wherever you specify you would like an effect. HTML generally works by inserting an opening code where you want special formatting to begin, and a closing code where you want it to end. For example, the following line of text (formatted using HTML) shows the word *abracadabra* in italic text.

Twirl your wand and say *abracadabra*!

If you were to look at the HTML source, it would look like this:

Twirl your wand and say <I>abracadabra</I>!

As you can see, the HTML tags that indicate italic text (**<I>** and **</I>**) surround *abracadabra*. The opening code, **<I>**, indicates where the italic text begins, and the closing code, **</I>**, indicates where it ends.

Internet Assistant hides the HTML details while you are creating an HTML document so you can have the pleasant experience of working with something that looks like a regular Word document. While this is one of Internet Assistant's best features, knowing a bit about how HTML works will help you understand what you are actually doing when you create Web documents. For that reason, I recommend that you take advantage of Internet Assistant's View HTML Source option often.

With that said, let's get started!

  Before you begin, copy two HTML files, *about.htm* and *catalog.htm*, from the CD to the My Documents folder on your hard drive.

Opening an Existing HTML Document

Let's begin by opening the home page you created in Lesson 3. It is stored in the My Documents folder on your hard drive.

  If you ever "lose" a file that you've previously created (you can't remember where it's stored on your hard drive), you can find it using the search fields at the bottom of the Open dialog box.

1 If it's not already open, launch Word by clicking on the **Start** button and selecting **Microsoft Word.**

► Word opens and presents you with a blank document.

2 Select **File ➢ Open.**

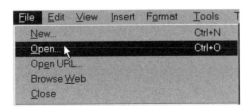

The Open dialog box appears and displays the contents of your My Documents folder. Here is your home page (*home. htm*) and the two HTML files you just copied from the CD (*about.htm* and *cata-log.htm*). If these file names aren't visible, make sure that the All files (*.*) option is selected in the File(s) of type field.

3 Double-click on **home.htm.**

 At this point, one of two things happens. If your Word settings do *not* include the "Confirm Conversion at Open" option (I'll explain what that is in a moment), *home.htm* will open as usual and you can skip the remaining steps in this section. If your Word settings *do* include this option, the Open dialog box disappears and the Convert File dialog box appears. Since you are using Word to open a file type other than a regular Word file (which has the file name extension *.doc*), the Convert File dialog box appears in order to confirm which type of document you are opening. Word recognizes the *.htm* file name extension and automatically highlights the HTML Document option.

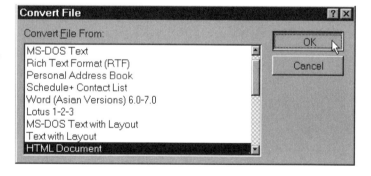

4 Click on the **OK** button
to open *home.htm*.

▶ The file *home.htm* opens.
Since it is an HTML docu-
ment, Word automatically
switches to HTML Edit
view, as you can see by
the change in the toolbars.

Marvin's Magic Shoppe

Welcome to Marvin's! Marvin is proud to be your guide through the dazzling world of magic.

About Marvin's

Catalog of Wares

Tell Marvin What You Think

▶ ▶ ▶ The Confirm Conversion at Open option is helpful if you routinely work
with lots of different file formats and want to be in control of how Word
handles the file conversion when it opens the file. For most people, however, this option is unnecessary. Word knows how to open the most commonly used file formats, including HTML files (thanks to Internet Assistant!). To turn off the Confirm Conversion at Open option, select Tools ➤
Options. The Options dialog box appears. Click on the General tab at the
top of the dialog box to display that set of options. Click on the Confirm
Conversion at Open check box to unmark it, and click on the OK button.
(The rest of the examples in this book will assume you've turned this
option off.)

Your home page is now ready for an HTML makeover!

Adding Pizzazz with Text Variation

Varying the look of the text in your Web pages makes it easier to read and more appealing
to the eye. You can use text variation to help organize information, call out important points
you wish to highlight, and make your pages look polished and professional (or hip and
stylish, depending on the image you'd like to project).

Internet Assistant makes varying your document's text simple; you get to take advantage
of Word's toolbars and a well-organized menu system.

▶ ▶ ▶ **I**nternet Assistant includes built-in support for several of Internet Explorer's and Netscape's HTML extensions (I discussed browser-specific extensions to HTML in Lesson 2). While this is exciting news for creative Web publishers, remember that some of your readers will be using Web browsers that *don't* display these extensions (including Internet Assistant's Web Browse view). Their browsers will simply ignore the extensions and display only those HTML tags they recognize, making your special effects nonexistent on their screens. Don't take this as advice *not* to use HTML extensions; just keep it in mind as you design your pages. I will call your attention to browser-specific extensions with notes as we go along.

Using the Formatting Toolbar

There are several HTML text formatting tools available on the Formatting toolbar. These tools allow you to make text bold, italic, or underlined, and to change the size of the font. We'll start by using the *Bold* and *Increase Font Size* tools.

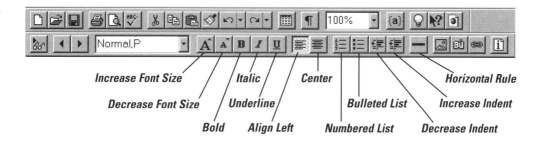

▶ ▶ ▶ **C**hanges in font size are an extension to HTML and will not be visible in all Web browsers.

1 In the second line of text on the home page, double-click on the word **dazzling** to highlight it.

the dazzling world of magic.

2 In the Formatting toolbar, click on the **Bold** button.

▶ The word *dazzling* turns bold.

the **dazzling** world of magic.

3 Using your cursor, high-light the words **Welcome to Marvin's!**.

Marvin's Magic Shoppe

Welcome to Marvin's!

4 Click on the **Increase Font Size** button.

▶ The font size of the phrase *Welcome to Marvin's!* increases by one increment.

Marvin's Magic Shoppe

Welcome to Marvin's!

And it's as easy as that.

▶ ▶ ▶ **How Font Size Works in HTML**

While font sizes in print documents are based on absolute measures such as points or picas, font size changes in HTML are based on a relative system of *increments*. In HTML, font sizes range in increments from 1 to 7, with 1 being the smallest and 7 being the largest. What this size turns out to be in points depends upon how the reader's Web browser interprets size tags. In Internet Assistant, the default font size (referred to in HTML as *basefont*) is 3, which is displayed on screen as 12-point type. When you change the font size by using the Increase Font Size command, you

(continued)

simply increase the basefont size by one increment, making it 4 instead of 3. In Internet Assistant, this will increase the size of the text to the next increment in the list of available font sizes, and it will be displayed as 14-point type.

Using the Style Menu

There are many more HTML text variations available than those displayed in the toolbar. The Address style, for example, is an HTML style that is traditionally used to display the address of the caretaker of a website. It's customary to include it at the bottom of the home page so that readers can reach the author or system administrator if they have questions or comments about the website. The address itself is usually a *snail-mail address* (Net-speak for street address) and/or an e-mail address.

► ► ►

Physical vs. Logical Styles

HTML has styles built into it (such as the Address style) that specify less what the text will actually *look like* once it's seen through a Web browser, and more what the text *means.* In HTML lingo, this difference is referred to as *physical* vs. *logical* styles. Physical styles affect the actual look of the text. Logical styles are used to indicate the meaning or content of the text, or to display certain types of standard text (such as addresses, for example). Remember, the Web browser is responsible for translating HTML formatting into the actual style you see when you look at a Web page. Some browsers may translate the Address style into italicized text (this is most common), while others may translate it as bold text of a smaller size. For that reason, using the Address style guarantees that every browser, while it may display addresses differently than other browsers, at least displays all addresses the same way.

Other logical styles included in Internet Assistant's HTML style list include Cite, Code, Emphasis, Sample, Strong, and Variable. To see how they appear in most Web browsers, refer to the HTML/Word Equivalents section of the Internet Assistant Help system.

Let's add Marvin's address to the bottom of the home page.

1 Using your mouse, place the cursor at the bottom of the page by clicking right after the word **Think.**

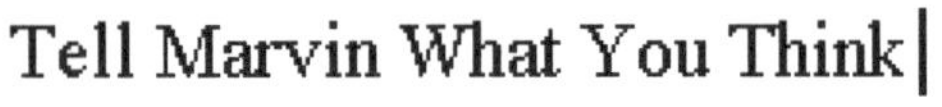

Tell Marvin What You Think|

2 Press ↵ to create a new line.

3 Type **Marvin's Magic Shoppe**, press **Shift-↵**, type **1000 Main Street**, press **Shift-↵**, type **Funplace, USA 10101**, and press **Shift-↵**.

Marvin's Magic Shoppe
1000 Main Street
Funplace, USA 10101|

▶ By the way, you typed Shift-↵ here instead of ↵ because Shift-↵ inserts a line break with no extra space around it, while ↵ creates an entirely new paragraph, which does have extra space around it.

Drag the cursor from here…

4 Highlight the text you just typed.

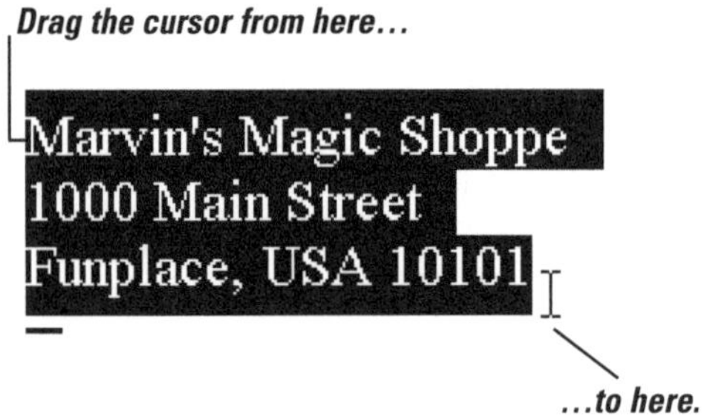

Marvin's Magic Shoppe
1000 Main Street
Funplace, USA 10101

…to here.

5 Select **Format** > **Style.**

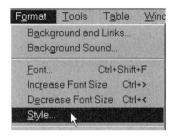

▶ The Style dialog box appears.

There is a lot to notice here. The Styles box lists all of the HTML styles you have available, and as you can see, there are quite a few. The "<u>a</u>" or "¶" that precedes the style name tells you if it is a character or paragraph style (character styles are applicable to individual characters in a document, while paragraph styles are only applicable to entire paragraphs).

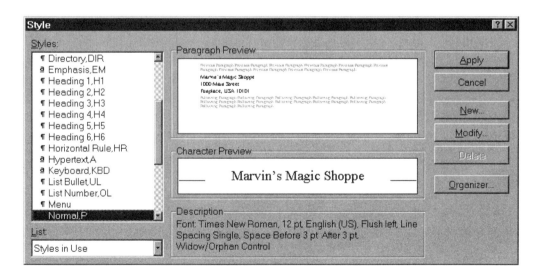

The Paragraph Preview and Character Preview boxes let you see what text in the highlighted style will look like once it's placed in your document (in this case, the normal Paragraph style is displayed). The Description box lists all of the style's font and paragraph format specifics. The List box controls which styles are displayed in the Styles box: the ones currently in use (in this case, the styles included in the *html.dot* template), user-defined styles (ones you've created on your own), or all styles.

6 Click on the scroll bar in the Styles box and drag it upward until the Address style is visible.

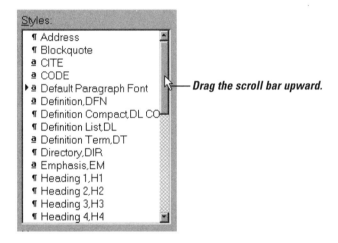

Drag the scroll bar upward.

7 Click on **Address.**

▶ Notice how the style of the text in the Character Preview box has changed. This is what the Address style looks like when viewed in Internet Assistant's Web Browse view.

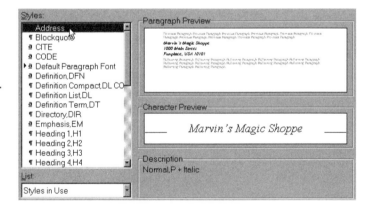

8 Click on the **Apply** button.

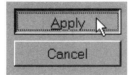

▶ The Style dialog box disappears, and the Address style is applied to the highlighted text.

Marvin's Magic Shoppe
1000 Main Street
Funplace, USA 10101

▶ ▶ ▶ **T**here are many more HTML styles available for you to use to enhance your Web pages (too many, in fact, to list examples of each one here). Instead, refer to the Internet Assistant Help system. The section entitled "HTML/Word Equivalents" includes a table that describes each HTML style that Internet Assistant supports.

▶ ▶ ▶ **T**he Style dialog box includes options that allow you to modify HTML styles and create new ones, but new and/or modified styles will only affect how the text appears on your screen when you use Internet Assistant to create HTML documents and browse the Web. They will *not* change the way your HTML documents appear when viewed on other computers with Internet Assistant, or when viewed with other Web browsers.

Using the Font Command

The *Font* command allows you even more control over the appearance of the text in your HTML documents. Using the Font command, you can:

- Select your document's font
- Change text color (down to individual characters)
- Change the size of characters using point size as a reference
- Define characters as superscript or subscript

Using the Font command is as easy as highlighting the text you want to format, selecting Format ➤ Font, and clicking on the option you'd like to use. For that reason, I'll illustrate each capability of the Font command, but we'll apply only one to Marvin's website: changing font color.

  All changes made with the Font command are extensions to HTML, and will not be visible in all Web browsers.

Selecting Your Document's Font

Internet Assistant lets you use any font that is stored in your computer's font directory in your Web pages. This is great news for Web publishers, since the right choice of font can lend a distinctive "feel" to documents. There is a big catch, however: as of this writing, typeface variations are visible only to those of your readers using one of Microsoft's Web browsers (Internet Explorer or Internet Assistant's Web Browse view). For everyone else, the regular body text in your documents will appear in whatever default font their browser displays (usually Times New Roman). Still, you may decide to take advantage of this feature, if only to give some of your readers a little treat.

You can use as many fonts as you like in an HTML document (just as in a regular Word document). The font (or fonts) you choose, however, must be present on your readers' computers for them to be visible on their screens. If the font isn't present, the text will be displayed in their browser's default font.

▶ ▶ ▶ **Y**ou can list several fonts as alternatives in case your first choice is not available on your reader's computer. To do so, you must edit the document's HTML source (I will show you how in Lesson 9).

To apply a font to a section of text (whether it is a character, word, paragraph, or entire page):

1 Highlight the text you'd like to format.

2 Select **Format** ➢ **Font**.

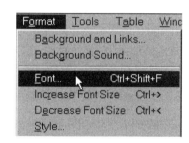

▶ The Font dialog box appears.

3 Choose a font from the Font drop-down list.

4 Click on the **OK** button.

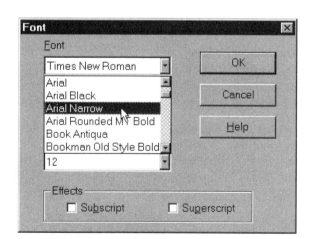

Changing Text Color

The Font command allows you control text color down to the character. You could conceivably give each letter in a word (or sentence or page) a different color (not that you would *want* to, of course!).

Let's add some color to Marvin's home page.

1 Highlight the words **Welcome to Marvin's!**.

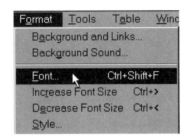

2 Select **Format > Font.**

▶ The Font dialog box appears.

3 Click on the **Color** drop-down list to display its contents.

4 Select **Red.**

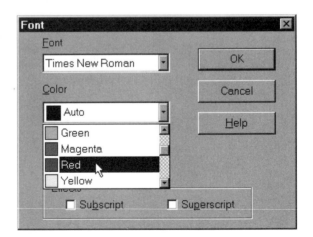

5 Click on the **OK** button.

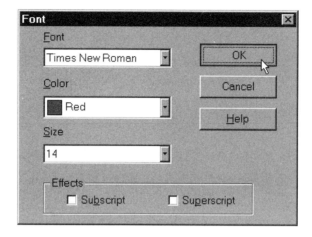

► The highlighted text turns red.

Marvin's Magic Shoppe

Welcome to Marvin's!

Changing Font Size

You've already had some experience with changing font size; you've seen the Increase Font Size tool in action earlier in this lesson. Using the Font command to change font size has the same effect. The only difference is that you can select the point size of the font as you would like it to be displayed, rather than simply increasing or decreasing it by increments.

► ► ► **E**ven though this command uses point size as a reference, the HTML source behind it is still based on the increment system (that is, 12-point type is of size 3). Point sizes are only guaranteed to be accurate when viewing documents with Internet Assistant or Internet Explorer because other Web browsers may assign different point values to each increment.

To change the size of a section of text:

1 Highlight the text you'd like to format.

2 Select **Format ➤ Font.**

▶ The Font dialog box appears.

3 Choose a font size from the Size drop-down list.

4 Click on the **OK** button.

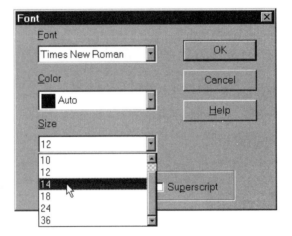

Superscript and Subscript

Footnotes and mathematical notations are two examples that use *superscript* and *subscript* text to convey important information. Superscript text appears slightly above regular text, and subscript text appears slightly below (the *x*s below illustrate the placement of superscript and subscript text).

$$\text{Superscript}^x \qquad \text{Subscript}_x$$

To define text as superscript or subscript:

1 Highlight the text you'd like to format.

2 Select **Format** ➤ **Font**.

▶ The Font dialog box appears.

3 Click on the **Superscript** or **Subscript** check box.

4 Click on the **OK** button.

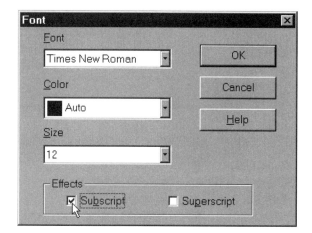

Using Headings to Organize Information

Headings call out important text in your document, such as page banners and categories. HTML lets you use six levels of headings, with 1 being the boldest and 6 the most modest. Traditionally, you use larger headings (such as Levels 1 and 2) for things such as page banners and important categories, saving the smaller heads (such as Levels 3–6) for lesser categories.

▶ ▶ ▶ **M**ind you, this is only the *traditional* way to use headings. Many Web publishers flout tradition when it comes to designing their pages. Remember, your home page is your creation. Use headings (and any other formatting effect) any way you like!

Let's use headings to help organize the information in your home page.

1 Using your cursor,
highlight the words
Marvin's Magic Shoppe
at the top of your
home page.

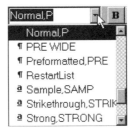

▶ Since this is the banner
of the home page, it
deserves the boldest
heading. Let's use the
Formatting toolbar as a
shortcut to the list of styles.

2 Click on the down-arrow
in the Style box to display
the list of available styles.

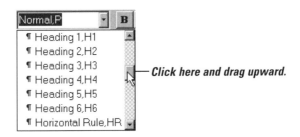

3 Click on the scroll bar
and drag it upward until
the Heading 1, H1 style
is visible.

— Click here and drag upward.

4 Click on **Heading 1, H1.**

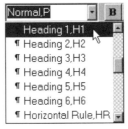

▶ The list disappears, and the Heading 1 style is applied to the highlighted text.

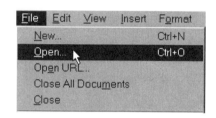

There. The home page banner now looks very important—as it should.

To see how headings can help prioritize information, let's apply two different levels of headings to the About Marvin's page (one of the HTML files you copied from the CD). The About Marvin's page tells the story of Marvin, the founder of Marvin's Magic Shoppe, and includes some other informational tidbits about his business.

1 Select **File** ➤ **Open**.

▶ The Open dialog box appears.

2 Double-click on **about.htm.**

▶ The About Marvin's page opens.

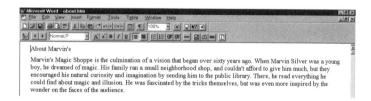

3 Using your cursor, highlight the words **About Marvin's.**

▶ Since this is the page banner, it makes good design sense to select the same level of heading as we did for the home page banner.

4 In the Style box, select **Heading 1, H1.**

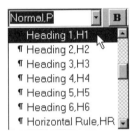

▶ Heading 1 is applied to the highlighted text.

We'll now use a smaller heading to highlight the secondary categories in this document. This emphasizes them while making it clear that they are not of the same importance as the page banner.

1 Click on the gray area of the scroll bar to move the viewing area of the document toward the bottom of the page.

— *Click here.*

2 Highlight the words **What is magic?**.

3 In the Style box, select **Heading 3, H3.**

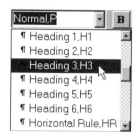

▶ Heading 3 is applied to the highlighted text.

What is magic?

magic: Any mysterious, seemingly inexplicable, or extraordinary power or quality

illusion: Something that appears to be what it's not

4 Highlight the words **Where can I find out more about magic on the Internet?**.

Where can I find out more about magic on the Internet?

5 In the Style box, select **Heading 3, H3.**

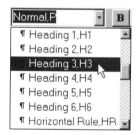

▶ Heading 3 is applied to the highlighted text.

Where can I find out more about magic on the Internet?

Marvin encourages you to visit Magic Central, a wonderful Internet resource devoted to magic lovers all over the world.

As you can see, using different levels of headings makes it easier for your readers to understand how the information in your pages is organized.

► ► ► **Y**ou can use the Format Painter (the button on the Standard toolbar that looks like a paintbrush) to quickly apply a style to other locations in your document. To do so, select the paragraph that has the style you want to copy. Click on the Format Painter button. A little paintbrush will appear next to your cursor letting you know the Format Painter is active. Select the paragraph you want to apply the style to, and presto, it's done! To copy the selected style to several locations, double-click on the Format Painter, select the paragraphs you want to format, and click on it again when you're finished.

While headings allow you to highlight categories and banners, lists allow you to organize the content of your Web pages.

Creating Lists

Lists tend to make themselves apparent in just about every Web page—after all, they are an easy and logical way to display similar types of information in a group. You can use Internet Assistant to create several kinds of lists. Let's add three different types of lists to your Web pages: a bulleted list (called an *unordered list* in HTML lingo), a numbered list (called an *ordered list*), and a definition list. We'll also modify a bulleted list to include more than one level of content (creating what is known as a *nested list*).

To demonstrate how to create and add lists, we'll use the other HTML document that was included on the CD, the Catalog of Wares page (*catalog.htm*). This page contains a sample listing of the products that are for sale at Marvin's.

Adding Bullets

Bulleted, or unordered, lists are a good way to display information that is of the same type.

1 Select **File** ➢ **Open**.

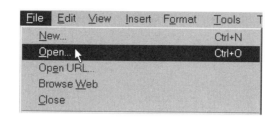

▶ The Open dialog box appears.

2 Double-click on **catalog.htm**.

▶ The Catalog of Wares page opens. As you can see, each category of product is followed by a list of items. In the case of the Magic Wands category, each item in the list (not surprisingly) is a different type of wand. Since the list contains similar—but distinct—products, it is perfectly suited to be accentuated with bullets, since the order of the list isn't important.

Catalog of Wares

Here is a small sampling of what you will find at Marvin's.

Magic Wands

The Apprentice: the perfect model for the beginner. Light, durable, and versatile.

The Magician: this wand provides more control for the experienced magician.

The Sorcerer: our deluxe model, this wand can make even large objects disappear.

3 Highlight the entire list of items that follows the category heading *Magic Wands*.

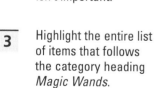

4 In the Formatting toolbar, click on the **Bulleted List** button (or, from the Style box, select **List Bullet, UL**).

5 The List Bullet style (called *UL* in HTML) is applied to the highlighted text.

Magic Wands

- The Apprentice: the perfect model for the beginner. Light, durable, and versatile.
- The Magician: this wand provides more control for the experienced magician.
- The Sorcerer: our deluxe model, this wand can make even large objects disappear.

The list of items really stands out now, whereas before it blended in with the rest of the text on the page. Now let's create a numbered list.

Adding Numbers

Numbered lists are useful when the order of the list contents is important. For example, the steps in this book have to be performed in a specific order; hence, they are numbered. Another reason to use numbered lists is to differentiate between items that are not equivalent, as they are in bulleted lists. For example, the next category, *Accessories,* contains items which are all different and would benefit by being distinguished from each other with the use of numbers.

1 Highlight the entire list of items that follows the category heading *Accessories.*

Accessories

Padded, upholstered table: the painless way to saw your assistant in half.

Flowing capes: they give you all the mystery a magician requires.

Top hats: fit all average-sized bunnies (best suited to floppy-eared varieties).

2 In the Formatting toolbar, click on the **Numbered List** button (or, from the Style box, select **List Number, OL**).

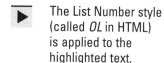 The List Number style (called *OL* in HTML) is applied to the highlighted text.

Accessories

1. Padded, upholstered table: the painless way to saw your assistant in half.
2. Flowing capes: they give you all the mystery a magician requires.
3. Top hats: fit all average-sized bunnies (best suited to floppy-eared varieties)

Creating a Nested List

Let's say you have a list (bulleted or numbered) that is more like an outline: it has categories and subcategories. You can choose to create a multilevel, or nested, list. For example, two of the items on our list of Card Tricks, the Beginner's deck and the Deluxe deck, are actually two different models of the Double-Decker. Let's make this clear by using a nested list.

1 Using your cursor, highlight the entire list of items that follows the category heading *Card Tricks*.

Card Tricks

The Double-Decker: a must-have for true card trick aficionados

Beginner's deck: a good first deck

Deluxe deck: for experts only

The Auto-Reshuffler: you'll never have to shuffle again

The Disappearing Jack: amaze your friends with this classic trick

2 In the Formatting toolbar, click on the **Bulleted List** button.

The List Bullet style is applied to the highlighted text.

Card Tricks

- The Double-Decker: a must-have for true card trick aficionados
- Beginner's deck: a good first deck
- Deluxe deck: for experts only
- The Auto-Reshuffler: you'll never have to shuffle again
- The Disappearing Jack: amaze your friends with this classic trick

3 Highlight the second and third items on the list: **Beginner's deck** and **Deluxe deck.**

Card Tricks

- The Double-Decker: a must-have for true card trick aficionados
- Beginner's deck: a good first deck
- Deluxe deck: for experts only
- The Auto-Reshuffler: you'll never have to shuffle again
- The Disappearing Jack: amaze your friends with this classic trick

4 In the Formatting toolbar, click on the **Increase Indent** button (or select **Format** ➤ **Increase Indent**).

▶ The highlighted items are indented.

Card Tricks

- The Double-Decker: a must-have for true card trick aficionados
    - Beginner's deck: a good first deck
    - Deluxe deck: for experts only
- The Auto-Reshuffler: you'll never have to shuffle again
- The Disappearing Jack: amaze your friends with this classic trick

There! Nesting has clarified the organization of the list, making it easy for readers to understand what kinds of card tricks they can choose from.

▶ ▶ ▶ **T**o "un-nest" items in a nested list, highlight those items and click on the Decrease Indent button.

▶ ▶ ▶ **I**n Internet Assistant, the Increase Indent and Decrease Indent tools *only* affect nested lists. If you use them for any other purpose (such as indenting a regular paragraph, for example), the formatting will have no effect on your finished Web page. To create an indented paragraph, use the Blockquote style instead.

▶ ▶ ▶ **I**nternet Assistant's Multilevel numbering command (in the Format menu) contains options that allow you to change the shape and format of bullets, numbers, and nested lists. I don't demonstrate it here, because not only are any changes you make invisible to other Web browsers, they don't exist the next time you open your HTML document in Internet Assistant (even if you save the changes before you close the document).

Creating a Definition List

A *definition list* is another way to display information in your Web pages. It's useful when you have terms you would like to explain.

Internet Assistant displays definition lists in two columns: on the left is the term to be defined and on the right, the definition. Most other browsers display it differently—usually with the definitions indented underneath the terms.

Let's add a definition list to the About Marvin's page.

1 Select **Window** ➢ **about.htm.**

▶ The About Marvin's page appears.

2 Click on the scroll bar to move the viewing area of the document toward the bottom of the page.

▶ Here we find perfect definition list material: the words *magic* and *illusion*, and their definitions. To format them, we must first separate the terms from their definitions with a tab character.

What is magic?

magic: Any mysterious, seemingly inexplicable, or extraordinary power or quality

illusion: Something that appears to be what it's not

Click here.

3 Using your mouse, place the cursor directly before the word **Any.**

What is magic?

magic: Any mysterious, seemingly inexplicable, or extraordinary power or quality

illusion: Something that appears to be what it's not

4 Press the **Tab** key to insert a tab.

▶ Don't worry about the placement of the text when you insert the tab; once we apply the definition list, the spacing will even out.

5 Place the cursor directly before the word **Something.**

What is magic?

magic: Any mysterious, seemingly inexplicable, or extraordinary power or quality

illusion: Something that appears to be what it's not

Click here.

6 Press the **Tab** key to insert a tab.

7   Highlight the entire list.

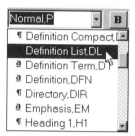

8   From the Style box, select **Definition List, DL.**

▶   The Definition List style (called *DL* in HTML) is applied to the highlighted text.

  ▶ ▶ ▶   **T**he Definition Compact, DC style looks just like the regular Definition List style when viewed in Internet Assistant, except it is slightly more compact. When viewed in other browsers, however, the two styles look identical.

Bulleted, numbered, nested, and definition lists aren't the only ones available to you. Others include the *menu* list (which is basically the same as a bulleted list) and the *directory* list (which is displayed by Internet Assistant in three columns and by most other browsers as a bulleted list). I'll leave those to you to experiment with if you feel like it.

Inserting Special Characters and Symbols

Pages written in HTML are, on a basic level, plain text files with special tags sprinkled throughout. Because they are plain text, some of the fancy characters you can type in your word processor (© for example) don't translate. The good news is that you can still use many of these special characters—you just need to do a little extra legwork.

HTML has tags for many special characters that look strange when viewed as HTML source, but when viewed through a browser, display the character you want. For example, the tag for the © symbol (below left) looks esoteric, but when viewed using Internet Explorer (below right), it assumes its familiar form.

Don't worry, you don't have to start memorizing strange codes to use special characters in your Web pages. Internet Assistant does it for you. Let's insert a special character into your Web pages by adding a copyright notice to the bottom of the home page.

▶ ▶ ▶ It's a good idea to put a copyright notice on all of your HTML documents in order to protect your original material once it's published on the Web.

1 Select **Window** ➢ **home.htm** to move to the home page.

2 Place the cursor at the bottom of the page by clicking right after the number **10101.**

Marvin's Magic Shoppe
1000 Main Street
Funplace, USA 10101 I

Click here.

3 Press the ↵ key to create a new line.

4 Select **Insert** ➤ **Symbol**.

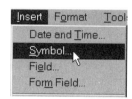

Click here.

The Symbol dialog box appears. Here you can choose which special character you would like to insert into your page. Notice there are two tabs to choose from: Symbols and Special Characters.

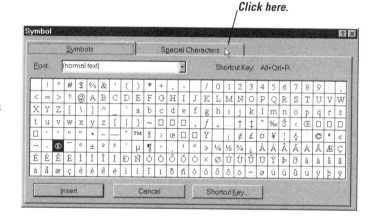

5 Click on the **Special Characters** tab at the top of the dialog box to make that option visible.

6 Double-click on © **Copyright**.

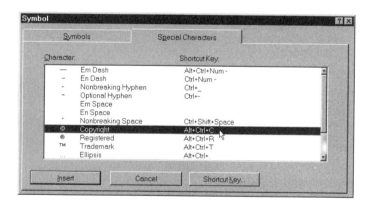

A © symbol appears on your home page.

Marvin's Magic Shoppe
1000 Main Street
Funplace, USA 10101

©

7 Click on the **Close** button of the Symbol dialog box.

▶ The Symbol dialog box disappears. Now, let's add the remainder of the copyright notice.

8 Type **Marvin's Magic Shoppe, 1999.**

Marvin's Magic Shoppe
1000 Main Street
Funplace, USA 10101

© Marvin's Magic Shoppe, 1999

▶ Since the copyright notice is something to which you don't want to call a lot of attention, it makes sense to format it with a smaller sized font.

9 Highlight the copyright notice.

© Marvin's Magic Shoppe, 1999

10 In the Formatting toolbar, click on the **Decrease Font Size** button.

▶ The font size of the copy-right notice decreases by one increment.

Marvin's Magic Shoppe
1000 Main Street
Funplace, USA 10101

© Marvin's Magic Shoppe, 1999

▶ ▶ ▶ If you would like to use the character choices in the Symbol dialog box, you must select (normal text) in the Font field for them to be correctly translated into HTML.

Changing Paragraph Alignment

The alignment tools in the Formatting toolbar allow you to left-align or center paragraphs with the click of a mouse.

Let's center the banner on Marvin's home page.

1 Highlight the words **Marvin's Magic Shoppe.**

2 Click on the **Center** button.

▶ The page banner is centered on the page.

Marvin's Magic Shoppe

Welcome to Marvin's! Marvin is proud to be your guide through the **dazzling** world of magic.

About Marvin's

Catalog of Wares

Tell Marvin What You Think

3 On your own, center the banners in *about.htm* and *catalog.htm* so that all three pages have a consistent design (I won't go through all the examples since you now have the hang of it).

 ▶ ▶ ▶ **S**hortcuts to several of the formatting options I've mentioned are available by clicking the rightmost button on your mouse. Depending upon where you click, a pop-up menu will appear, giving you instant access to different HTML formatting options.

Adding a Horizontal Rule

Typeface variation, headings, and lists are all good ways to organize and present information. Another option is to use a *horizontal rule.*

A horizontal rule is a solid line that runs the width of your Web page, similar to a bottom border in Word. You can insert rules anywhere you would like to separate different types of information or add some variety. I find that adding a rule underneath the page banner creates a good break between it and the rest of the page. Let's add a horizontal rule to your home page.

1 Place the cursor directly before the word **Welcome.**

Welcome to Marvin's!

Click here.

2 In the Formatting toolbar, click on the **Horizontal Rule** button (or select **Insert ➤ Horizontal Rule**).

▶ A horizontal rule appears underneath the home page banner. As you can see, the simple addition of a horizontal rule adds nice variety to your page.

Marvin's Magic Shoppe

Welcome to Marvin's! Marvin is proud to be your guide through the **dazzling** world of magic.

3 On your own, add horizontal rules above Marvin's address on the home page and underneath the page banners of *about.htm* and *catalog.htm.*

Previewing Your Document in Another Web Browser

While you are creating an HTML document, it's a good idea to view it with a Web browser to see what it will look like once it's "live" and available for public viewing on the Web. That way, you can make design modifications as you go along to make sure the page will look the way you want once it's online. Internet Assistant's interface approximates how your page will look on the Web, but because it can't display all of the features it can create as a Web publishing tool, you are better off previewing your document in another, more powerful browser such as Internet Explorer.

The creators of Internet Assistant, being the thoughtful bunch they are, added a special button to the Standard toolbar that allows you to preview your document with one click. The Preview in Browser command (also available in the File menu) launches whatever Web browser you have installed on your computer and displays the document you are working on in another viewing window. In this case, Internet Explorer's icon is displayed on the button, since it's my default Web browser. If you use another browser, its icon will appear on the button.

Preview in Browser button

Once you preview the document in the browser, you can switch back to Internet Assistant to make any changes you like. To view the changes, save the document and return to the browser by clicking on its button in the Windows 95 Taskbar. If necessary, use the browser's Reload or Refresh command to display the latest version of your document.

► ► ► **B**e sure to use the program buttons in the Taskbar to move back and forth between Internet Assistant and your Web browser. If you use the Preview in Browser button after the browser has already been launched, it will open a second viewing window to display the changes in your document. While this is not a problem, it will clutter up your screen with lots of viewing windows that contain the same thing.

This feature is especially useful when you add elements to your HTML documents that are not accurately displayed by Internet Assistant, such as interactive forms, tables, and background colors. We'll use the Preview in Browser command when we work with these elements in Lessons 7, 8, and 9.

► ► ► **Y**ou may notice that your HTML documents look different once you save, close, and open them again in Internet Assistant (or when you view HTML source and return to HTML Edit view). Don't worry—this quirk is a normal function of Internet Assistant, and it doesn't affect the look of your page in another browser. If you're in doubt, use the Preview in Browser command to view your document. For details, consult the Internet Assistant Help system. Double-click on the Definitions and Common Questions heading; when the list of documents appears, double-click on Frequently asked questions for the answer to this and other common questions about Internet Assistant.

You've added lots of formatting to your pages in this lesson—time to take a break. Let's save all of the changes you've made and exit Word.

1 Select **File** ➤ **Exit.** (If you feel like moving on to the next lesson right now, you can skip this step; instead, select File ➤ Save All to save the changes you've made to your files.)

▶ The Microsoft Word dialog box appears, asking if you would like to save your document.

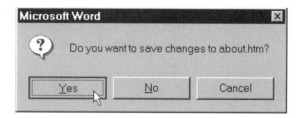

2 Click on the **Yes** button.

▶ The Save Format dialog box appears, reminding you that you're saving your documents in HTML format.

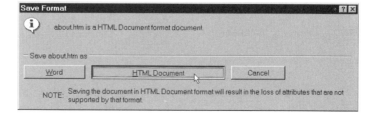

3 Click on the **HTML Document** button.

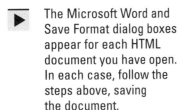 The Microsoft Word and Save Format dialog boxes appear for each HTML document you have open. In each case, follow the steps above, saving the document.

▶ Word saves your documents, shuts down, and your desktop reappears.

You've learned a lot in this lesson about HTML's formatting options and how to use Internet Assistant to apply them to your Web pages. In the next lesson, you'll start "weaving your web" by adding hyperlinks to your pages.

CREATING HYPERLINKS

In **Lesson 4,** you spruced up your Web pages with all kinds of HTML formatting effects. But, as we all know, the excitement of HTML isn't in its formatting prowess…it's in those little powerhouses called *hyperlinks.*

You experienced the power of hyperlinks during your surf session in Lesson 2—they are the blue, underlined bits of text within each Web page that, when clicked on, transport you to another location.

In this lesson, we'll add hyperlinks to your home page. We will use hyperlinks to jump to another location within a page. We'll link all of your pages together so that you (and your readers) can move among them with a single click. Finally, we'll weave your site into the fabric of cyberspace by hyperlinking it to another site on the Web.

Hyperlinks, like every other piece of HTML, are defined by tags that Internet Assistant inserts into your document. This is what the HTML source for a hyperlink looks like…

```
<A HREF="http://www.someplace.com/somefile.htm" >Hyperlink text goes here</A>
```
Opening tag   **Hypertext reference**   **Hyperlink text**   **Closing tag**

…and here is what it looks like when viewed through a Web browser.

<u>Hyperlink text goes here</u>

Like other HTML formatting, hyperlinks have an opening tag, **<A>**, and a closing tag, **</A>**, with the hyperlink text itself nestled in between. The rest of the tag consists of the *hypertext reference* (HREF for short). The hypertext reference is the link destination. In other words, it is the place to which readers will jump when they click on the hyperlink. That destination can be a location within the document they are viewing, a different HTML document stored on the server, or a document stored in a remote location on the Web. In the example above, clicking on the hyperlink would take you to the HTML document named *somefile.htm* located at the URL **http://www.someplace.com**.

 ▶ ▶ ▶ **E**ven though the destination of a hyperlink is called the *hypertext refer-ence,* it can refer to any number of file formats (not just text). For example, you can create a hyperlink to a graphic file, in which case the graphic will appear by itself on the viewer's screen when the link is activated.

Let's add some hyperlinks to your HTML documents.

Linking to Another Location within a Page

You can use hyperlinks to help you navigate a particularly long HTML document by using *bookmarks.* Bookmarks identify locations in your document that hyperlinks can jump to.

Let's add a bookmark to *about.htm.* We'll create a hyperlink at the top of the page that, when clicked on, will transport the reader to a bookmark at the bottom of the page.

1 Open Word by clicking on the **Start** button and selecting **Microsoft Word.**

▶ Word opens and presents you with a blank document.

2 Select **File** ➢ **Open.**

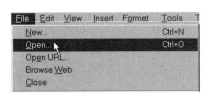

▶ The Open dialog box appears and displays the contents of your My Documents folder.

3 Double-click on **about.htm.**

The first step is to define the bookmark itself. The bookmark is the word that will eventually become the destination of the hyperlink.

4 Click on the scroll bar to move the viewing area of the document toward the bottom of the page.

5 Double-click on the word **magic** to highlight it.

What is magic?

magic: I   Any mysterious, seemingly inexplicable, or extraordinary power or quality

illusion: Something that appears to be what it's not

6 In the Formatting toolbar, click on the **Bookmark** button (or select **Edit ➢ Bookmark**).

▶ The Bookmark dialog box appears.

7 In the Bookmark Name field, type **magic.**

8 Click on the **Add** button.

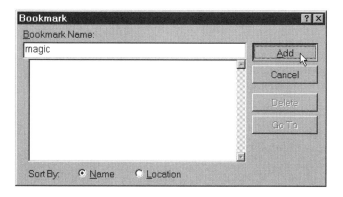

▶ The Bookmark dialog box disappears. The word *magic* is now defined as a bookmark. The next step is to define the text you want to transform into a hyperlink.

9 Scroll back toward the top of the document.

10 In the first paragraph, double-click on the word **magic** to highlight it.

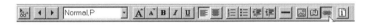

Marvin's Magic Shoppe is the boy, he dreamed of magic. His encouraged his natural curiosit

11 In the Formatting toolbar, click on the **Hyperlink** button.

▶ The Hyperlink dialog box appears. In the Text to Display field, Internet Assistant has filled in the word *magic* (this is the word you just highlighted). Now you will attach the hyperlink to its destination: the bookmark you just created.

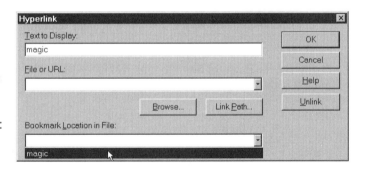

12 Click on the down-arrow on the right side of the **Bookmark Location in File** field.

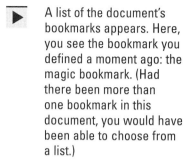

▶ A list of the document's bookmarks appears. Here, you see the bookmark you defined a moment ago: the magic bookmark. (Had there been more than one bookmark in this document, you would have been able to choose from a list.)

13 Select the **magic** bookmark.

14 Click on the **OK** button.

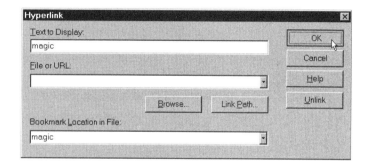

▶ The Hyperlink dialog box disappears, and the word *magic* is now displayed in blue, underlined text, letting you know that it has turned into a hyperlink.

Marvin's Magic Shoppe is the
boy, he dreamed of <u>magic</u>. His
encouraged his natural curiosit

15 Double-click on **magic** to activate the hyperlink.

Shoppe is the
of   . H
atural curios

▶ You jump to the location of the *magic* bookmark.

magic: Any mysterious, seemingly inexplicable, or extraordinary power or quality

illusion: Something that appears to be what it's not

Bookmarks are a great way to get around within a Web page. You can also jump *between* pages by using hyperlinks to link HTML documents together.

Linking to Your Own HTML Pages

Hyperlinks transform your website from a collection of separate documents to an integrated unit. Until now, you've been creating and modifying the individual components of your site. We'll now use hyperlinks to string those components together.

We'll do this in two ways: by adding hyperlinks to the home page (since its main purpose is to direct folks to the other pages in your site), and by creating a hypertext *menu bar* that will sit at the bottom of your other pages. A menu bar is a row of hyperlinks that connect to each page in your site, allowing readers to navigate your entire website easily. With a menu bar, your readers can jump to any page in your website from any other page; they don't have to return to the home page each time.

▶ ▶ ▶ **Relative vs. Absolute Hyperlinks**

Hyperlinks to other documents come in two flavors: *relative* and *absolute*. While the distinction is invisible when you are websurfing, it is important for you as a Web publisher to understand.

Relative hyperlinks express the destination relative to the location of the document the hyperlink is in. For example, take a look at the HTML source for the following link:

<A HREF="about.htm">About Marvin's</A>

Relative link to the file **about.htm**

As you can see, the hyperlink destination is simply the file name *about.htm*. When a Web browser encounters this hyperlink, it looks for the file *about.htm* in the same directory as the file that contains the hyperlink. If *about.htm* isn't there, the link won't work.

An absolute hyperlink contains the full URL of its destination. For example, look at HTML source for a hyperlink to Rob's Magic and Juggling Shop:

<A HREF="http://www.nmia.com/~magic">Rob's Magic and Juggling Shop</A>

Absolute link to the URL **http://www.nmia.com/~magic**

(continued)

When a Web browser encounters this kind of hyperlink, it goes straight to the destination URL, no matter where the original file is located.

While the difference between relative and absolute hyperlinks may seem too technical to worry about, it is central to the workings of your home page. You use relative hyperlinks when linking together documents you've created, because you control their location and can therefore create valid links. You use absolute hyperlinks when linking to URLs on the Web.

For more information on how and when to use relative versus absolute links, consult the Internet Assistant Help system.

Linking from Your Home Page

Let's begin with your home page. We'll create relative hyperlinks to the rest of your site, both to pages that already exist (the About Marvin's and the Catalog of Wares pages), and to a page we haven't yet created, but will add to the website in a later lesson.

1   Select **File ➢ Open.**

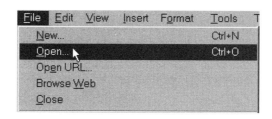

▶   The Open dialog box appears and displays the contents of the My Documents folder.

2   Double-click on **home.htm.**

▶   The home page opens.

3 Highlight the words **About Marvin's.**

4 Click on the **Hyperlink** button.

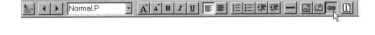

▶ The Hyperlink dialog box appears. As before, the selected text appears in the Text to Display field. This time, instead of linking to a bookmark, we'll create a relative link to another HTML file.

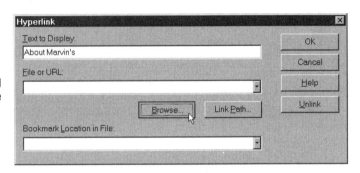

5 Click on the **Browse** button to display a list of file choices.

▶ The Select File to Link dialog box appears, and the contents of your My Documents folder are visible.

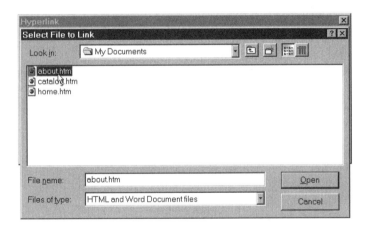

6 Double-click on **about.htm.**

▶ The Select File to Link dialog box disappears, and the Hyperlink dialog box becomes visible again. As you can see, *about.htm* appears in the File or URL field, indicating that you are creating a relative link to that file.

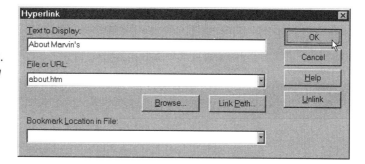

7 Click on the **OK** button.

▶ <u>About Marvin's</u> is now a hyperlink to *about.htm*.

About Marvin's

Catalog of Wares

Tell Marvin What You Think

8 Double-click on **About Marvin's** to activate the hyperlink.

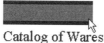

Catalog of Wares

Tell Marvin What You Think

▶ You jump to the About Marvin's page.

About Marvin's

Marvin's Magic Shoppe is the culmination of a vision that began over sixty years ago. When Marvin Silver was a young boy, he dreamed of magic. His family ran a small neighborhood shop, and couldn't afford to give him much, but they encouraged his natural curiosity and imagination by sending him to the public library. There, he read everything he could find about magic and illusion. He was fascinated by the tricks themselves, but was even more inspired by the wonder on the faces of the audience.

9 On your own, transform the next line in the home page, "Catalog of Wares," into a hyperlink to *catalog.htm*. Follow the same steps as you did above for *about.htm*, except choose the file *catalog.htm* as the hyperlink destination.

Now we'll create a hyperlink to a page in the website that doesn't yet exist. Why? Because often when you're building a website you do so in stages; you complete one part of the website while other parts haven't even been started. Creating hyperlinks to yet-to-be-finished documents allows you to wrap up one part of the website (in this case, the home page), so that when the other parts are ready, they simply need to be slipped into place.

1   If you aren't there already, return to the home page window by selecting **Window ➢ home.htm.**

2   Highlight the text **Tell Marvin What You Think.**

About Marvin's

Catalog of Wares

Tell Marvin What You Think

3   Click on the **Hyperlink** button.

▶   The Hyperlink dialog box appears. Since the destination file does not yet exist, you can't use the Browse button to select it—you must type in the name of the file.

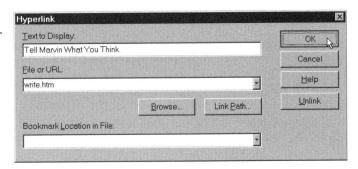

Hyperlink

Text to Display:
Tell Marvin What You Think

File or URL:
write.htm

Browse...   Link Path...

Bookmark Location in File:

OK
Cancel
Help
Unlink

4   In the File or URL field, type **write.htm.**

5   Click on the **OK** button.

▶ The Hyperlink dialog box disappears, and <u>Tell Marvin What You Think</u> is now a hyperlink to the nonexistent file *write.htm* (we'll create the file in Lesson 8).

<u>About Marvin's</u>

<u>Catalog of Wares</u>

<u>Tell Marvin What You Think</u>|

6 Double-click on **Tell Marvin What You Think**.

<u>About Marvin's</u>

<u>Catalog of Wares</u>

▶ Nothing happens, since the link is still incomplete. Once we create *write.htm* and place it in the same directory as *home.htm* (since this is a relative link, after all), the hyperlink will work perfectly.

  If you would like to unlink one of the hyperlinks you have created, select it, click on the Hyperlink button, and in the Hyperlink dialog box, click on the Unlink button. It will return to being plain text.

Linking from a Text Menu Bar

Websurfers appreciate thoughtfully placed hyperlinks that make it easy for them to find the information they want. The inclusion of a menu bar at the top or bottom (or, if the pages are very long, both) of your Web pages makes navigating your site easy and intuitive.

  Of course, the home page doesn't need a menu bar, since it is entirely devoted to leading readers to the rest of your site.

A menu bar contains hyperlinks to each page in your website. It can take the form of a line of text hyperlinks, a row of hyperlinked graphics, or an imagemap. We'll add a text menu bar to your pages. The process for creating it is the same as for the home page; we'll create relative links between the items in the menu bar and the pages in your site.

1 Select **Window** ➤ **about.htm.**

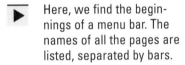

▶ The About Marvin's page appears.

2 Scroll toward the bottom of the page.

▶ Here, we find the beginnings of a menu bar. The names of all the pages are listed, separated by bars.

Home page | About Marvin's | Catalog of Wares | Write to Marvin

3 Highlight the words **Home page.**

Home page | About Marvin's | Catalog of Wares | Write to Marvin

4 Click on the **Hyperlink** button.

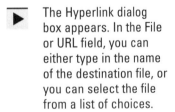

▶ The Hyperlink dialog box appears. In the File or URL field, you can either type in the name of the destination file, or you can select the file from a list of choices.

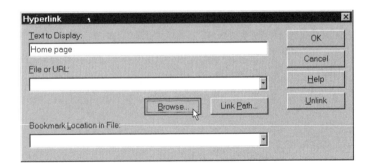

5 Click on the **Browse** button to display a list of file choices.

▶ The Select File to Link dialog box appears, and the contents of your My Documents folder are visible.

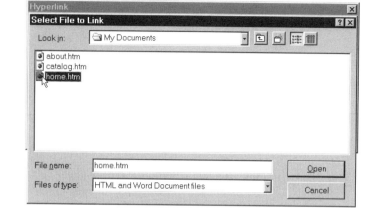

6 Double-click on **home.htm**.

▶ The Select File to Link dialog box disappears, and the Hyperlink dialog box becomes visible again. *home.htm* appears in the File or URL field, indicating that you are creating a relative link to that file.

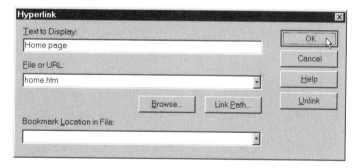

7 Click on the **OK** button.

▶ Home page is now a hyperlink to *home.htm*.

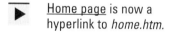

Home page | About Marvin's | Catalog of Wares | Write to Marvin

8 On your own, transform the other items in the menu bar into hyperlinks to their corresponding pages. Follow the same steps as you did for *home.htm* above, specifying the appropriate file names as hyperlink destinations.

In Lesson 10, we'll copy the menu bar and paste it into each of the pages of your website (since they will all be complete by then).

The Link Path Button Explained

You may have noticed another button in the Insert Hyperlink dialog box: the Link Path button. This button deserves a bit of explanation even though you may not have occasion to use it.

When you attempt to create a hyperlink in a new HTML document without having saved the document first, you will be presented with the following dialog box:

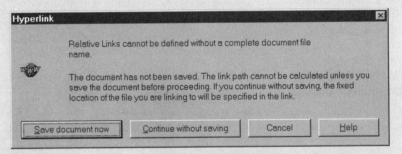

This dialog box tells you that, in order to create a relative link, you must first save the document (unless the document is saved, Internet Assistant has no reference point upon which to base its jump to the hyperlink destination).

The dialog box then allows you to save the document at that moment or continue the process of creating the hyperlink without saving the document. If you choose to save the file, you can create a relative link as usual (and you'll never have to give the Link Path button a second thought). If you choose *not* to save the document, you will still be able to create the hyperlink, but Internet Assistant, since it has no relative location information, will link to the *fixed file location*. That is, it will include the directory and drive location of the hyperlink destination file in the hyperlink reference.

(continued)

Here's an example of the difference between a relative and a fixed hyperlink. A working relative link to the About Marvin's page looks like this:

<A HREF="about.htm">About Marvin's</A>

A hyperlink to a fixed file location looks like this:

<A HREF="C:\My Documents\about.htm">About Marvin's</A>

As you can see, the fixed hyperlink includes the full location of the file *about.htm* on your computer's hard drive. Once the home page is transferred to the Web server (so it can be viewed by the public), the hyperlink will not work, since the file location information is now incorrect.

The remedy to this situation is the Link Path button. If you have created a hyperlink with a fixed file location, you can turn it into a relative link by selecting the hyperlink, clicking on the Hyperlink button, and then clicking on the Link Path button. By unmarking the Fixed File Location option, you can remove the location information from the hyperlink, turning it into a working relative link.

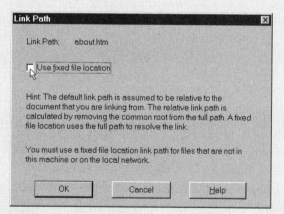

The moral of this story is that as long as you save your HTML documents before creating hyperlinks (or save the document when prompted by the dialog box), you can avoid this confusion entirely.

Linking to a Page Elsewhere on the Web

The essence of the Web's appeal is the ease with which you can hop from site to site, not having to think about whether the files are located down the street or across the world. As you will see, creating hyperlinks to documents that are located in remote places on the Web is just as easy as linking to documents of your own creation.

Let's create an absolute link from *about.htm* to another magic-related site on the Web.

 ► ► ► **Y**ou need to activate your Internet connection in order to follow the hyperlink we'll create in this section.

1 If they're not already visible, scroll up until you can see the words **Where can I find out more about magic on the Internet?**.

Where can I find out more about magic on the Internet?

Marvin encourages you to visit Magic Central, a wonderful Internet resource devoted to magic lovers all over the world.

► Marvin's isn't the only magic-related site on the Web. But since Marvin is a neighborly guy, he's happy to pass readers along to a resource that puts them in touch with other online magicians and magic shops.

2 Highlight the words **Magic Central.**

Marvin encourages you to visit

3 Click on the **Hyperlink** button.

▶ The Hyperlink dialog box appears. This time, instead of creating a relative link to a page we've created, we'll link to a URL on the Web.

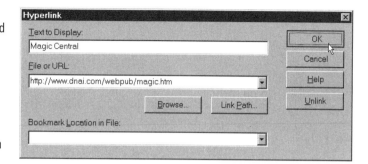

4 In the File or URL field, type **http://www.dnai.com /webpub/magic.htm**.

5 Click on the **OK** button.

▶ <u>Magic Central</u> is now a hyperlink to a location on the Web.

Marvin encourages you to visit <u>Magic Central</u>

6 Double-click on **Magic Central**.

Marvin encourages you to visit

▶ There is a momentary pause as Internet Assistant downloads the Magic Central home page.

7 The Magic Central website appears.

Magic Central

Your source for links to magic-related sites all over the Internet!

 ▶ ▶ ▶ Including links in your home page to sites of related interest is a nice way to "bid farewell" to your readers as they continue their Web journey. It also promotes a feeling of community among like-minded folks on the Web.

Wasn't that easy?

▶ ▶ ▶

Copying Hyperlinks

In the example above, I happened to have the URL of Magic Central handy. But let's say you are out websurfing using Internet Assistant's Web Browse view, and you come across a site whose URL you would like to add to your home page. Internet Assistant makes it easy—select Edit ➤ Copy HyperLink. Internet Assistant copies the URL to your clipboard, and you can then paste it (as a ready-made hyperlink) into your Web page.

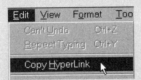

You can also copy hyperlinks from your History List. Display your History list, click on the URL you want to hyperlink, and click on the Copy HyperLink button. You can now paste the hyperlink into your Web page.

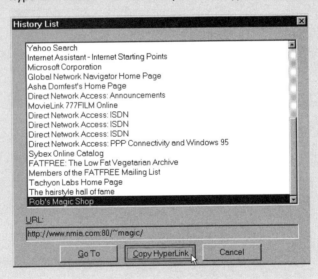

You've done a lot of good work on your home page (and you have lots of hyperlinks to show for it). Time to take a break.

1 Select **File ➢ Exit** and respond to the dialog boxes that appear, saving each of your files as HTML documents. (If you feel like moving on to the next lesson right now, you can skip this step; instead, select File ➢ Save All to save the changes you've made to your files.)

▶ Word saves your documents and shuts down. Your desktop reappears.

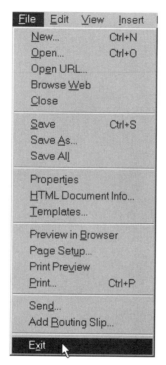

In this lesson, you've used hyperlinks to make it easy for your readers to navigate your website and to visit related sites on the Web. In the next lesson, we'll get jazzy by adding graphics to your site.

PART THREE

GETTING JAZZY

ADDING PICTURES TO YOUR WEB PAGES

Until now, we've focused on the content of your Web pages. After all, the purpose of a website is to provide information, and up-to-date information is what keeps new readers coming to your site and old ones coming back. But who says information can't be beautiful?

The Web's popularity comes from its easy-to-access storehouse of information combined with brilliant, full-color pictures. In this lesson, we'll use pictures to dress up your Web pages.

When you insert a picture in a Web page, you create what's called an *inline image*. An inline image is a reference within the document to the graphic file you would like to display in that location. When a Web browser encounters the inline image reference, it searches for the graphic file to which it refers, and displays it as part of the Web page.

On the left is the HTML source for an inline image, along with the HTML tag **<P>** (for Paragraph) and some regular text. On the right, you can see how the image and its corresponding text look when viewed through Internet Explorer.

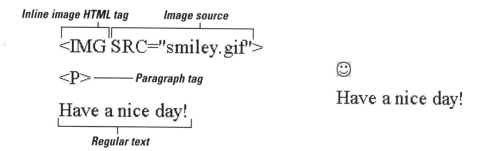

The inline image consists of the tag **<IMG>** and reference to the graphic file itself, called the *image source* (abbreviated **SRC**). The image source is the name and location of the file that is to be displayed in the HTML document (in this case, *smiley.gif*).

You may have noticed that the tag looks very much like the HTML source for a hyperlink. Like a hyperlink, its purpose is to connect two distinct files: the HTML file that contains the picture, and the graphic file itself. Also, the image source can be expressed as a relative link to a graphic file stored on the Web server, or as an absolute link to a graphic file located elsewhere on the Web.

Inline images must be in one of two file formats: *GIF* or *JPG*. These are the only graphic file formats Web browsers know how to display. GIF is the most commonly used format because it is universally recognized by graphical Web browsers. The JPG format is useful for especially large graphics, since it can pack more detail into a small file size (which allows JPG graphics to load faster than GIFs).

How do you know which format to use? Generally, the GIF format is used for all but the largest of graphics.

 ▶ ▶ ▶ **U**sing JPGs can be a bit tricky because older versions of some Web browsers can't display inline JPG graphics. The vast majority of your readers will be using one of the newer browsers, however, so 99 percent of the time it won't be a problem.

This brings up an important design issue. Pictures, while they give your site personality and color, significantly increase the time it takes to load. Most websurfers want to look at attractive, creatively designed pages, but they don't want to sit, tapping their fingers, while it downloads for 30 seconds or more. Remember, not all of your readers have access to lightning-fast Internet connections or state-of-the-art browsers. In fact, some of your readers won't even see the pictures because they have turned off image loading, or they are using a text-based browser that doesn't display pictures at all.

Here are some tips to help you balance the beauty and functionality of pictures in your website:

- Use pictures judiciously; include only those that will add to the overall impact or feel of your page.
- Specify the dimensions of each of your pictures (we'll talk about why later in the lesson).
- Limit the size of pictures in your web pages; small ones take less time to load than large ones.
- Limit the number of colors in your pictures; those with fewer colors load more quickly than those with many.
- Make sure that your page isn't totally dependent on pictures to make its point (remember, not all of your readers will see them).

Keeping these points in mind will help you design attractive, fast-loading pages your readers will appreciate.

Now that you have a sense for how inline images behave, let's add some to Marvin's Web pages.

  Before you begin, copy *logo.gif* and *gohome.gif* from the CD to the My Documents folder on your hard drive.

Inserting a Picture as an Illustration

Many well-designed websites begin with an opening picture—one that sets the tone for the rest of the site. In a business-related website, the company logo is the perfect choice. Let's insert Marvin's logo at the top of the home page.

1 Open Word by clicking on the **Start** button and selecting **Microsoft Word.**

▶ Word opens and presents you with a blank document.

2 Select **File** ➢ **Open**.

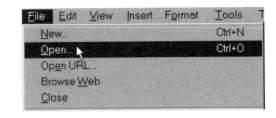

▶ The Open dialog box appears and displays the contents of your My Documents folder.

3 Double-click on **home.htm.**

▶ The home page opens.

4 Place the cursor at the top of the page by clicking directly in front of the heading **Marvin's Magic Shoppe.**

Marvin's Magic Shoppe

5 Press the ↵ key to put some space before the line of text.

6 Place the cursor back at the top of the page by clicking there with your mouse.

Marvin's Magic Shoppe

7 In the Formatting toolbar, click on the **Picture** button (or select **Insert ➤ Picture**).

▶ The Picture dialog box appears. This dialog box allows you to enter all of the details necessary to create an inline image. You specify the name and location of the graphic file in the Image Source field. As in the Hyperlink dialog box, there is a Browse button that allows you to create a relative link to a graphic by choosing among available GIF or JPG files on your hard drive. (There is also a Link Path button that serves the same purpose as in the Hyperlink dialog box.)

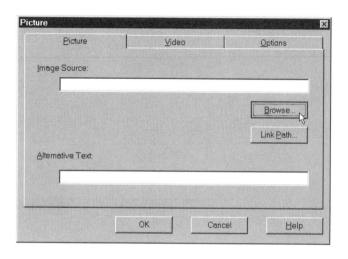

8 Click on the **Browse** button.

▶ The Insert Picture dialog box appears. On the left side of the dialog box is a diagram of the files and folders on your computer (in the illustration, the contents of Word's default graphics folder, the Clipart folder, are visible); on the right, a preview window that gives you a peek at graphic files before you open them; and at the bottom, a search function that allows you to find a particular file.

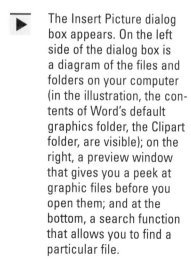

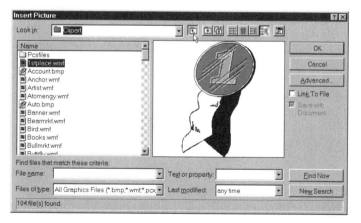

9 Click on the **Up One Level** button until the contents of your hard drive are visible.

10 Double-click on the **My Documents** folder to make its contents visible.

11 Double-click on **logo.gif.**

▶ The Insert Picture dialog box disappears, and the Picture dialog box becomes visible again. *logo.gif* appears in the Image Source field, which means that the inline image reference is now a relative link to the file *logo.gif.*

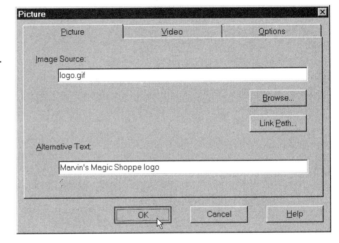

▶ Now, you need to specify the graphic's *alternative text.* Alternative text appears in place of pictures in cases where your readers have turned off image loading or are otherwise unable to view them. Alternative text allows your readers to get a sense of how the site looks with the pictures intact.

12 In the Alternative Text field, type **Marvin's Magic Shoppe logo.**

13 Click on the **OK** button.

▶ Marvin's logo appears in your home page.

Marvin's Magic Shoppe

What a difference! The addition of one picture has given new life to your home page!

▶ ▶ ▶ **E**ven though the Preview box in the Insert Picture dialog box can display many graphic file formats (giving you the impression that you can use them in your HTML documents), only GIF and JPG images will be visible in your Web pages.

▶ ▶ ▶ **Where Do I Find Pictures to Add to My Home Page?**

There are four ways to go about adding pictures to your website:

- You can create your own using commercial or shareware graphics software.

- You can buy collections of public-use clip art.

- You can convert pictures you already have into GIF or JPG files.

- You can go to one of the many clip art galleries on the Internet and copy pictures from there to your own computer for use in your Web pages.

(continued)

If you want to convert an existing graphic file such as a logo, Internet Assistant does the work for you. It contains an automatic GIF translator that springs into action as soon as you convert a Word document that contains a picture or OLE object into HTML. Internet Assistant converts them into GIFs and stores them in the same folder as the document. It also creates inline image references in the resulting HTML page. The images will be named *Img00001.gif, Img00002.gif,* etc. You can rename them with more intuitive file names at a later point, but be sure to update the image source in your document to reflect the new names as well.

You can also use a commercial or shareware graphics program to open your files individually and save them as GIF or JPG format. I include links to good shareware graphic converters in the Online Resource.

If you just want to add some spice to your website by tossing in a few colorful icons, there are "galleries" on the Internet that invite you to use their pictures in your site. The easiest way to use these pictures in your Web pages is to copy the ones you like to your computer's hard drive, and then insert them into your HTML document as usual. The Online Resource lists several of the Web's best clip art resources, as well as directions for copying pictures to your hard drive.

One word of caution: make sure that any graphics you borrow from commercial or public access collections have no copyrights attached. If they do, you must first obtain permission from the owner to use them in your website.

Inserting a Picture as a Hyperlink

Pictures can do more than just decorate. While you can use them as simple illustrations, you can also turn them into graphic hyperlinks. Your readers click directly on the picture, just as they would on a text hyperlink, to go to another location.

Let's replace one of the text hyperlinks in the menu bar with a graphic hyperlink.

1 Select **File** ➤ **Open.**

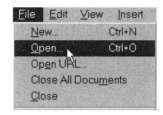

2 Double-click on **about.htm.**

▶ The About Marvin's page opens.

3 Scroll to the bottom of the page.

▶ The menu bar becomes visible.

4 Click on the **Home page** hyperlink to select it.

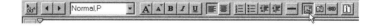

5 Press the **Delete** key to delete the hyperlink.

|| About Marvin's | Catalog of Wares | Write to Marvin
—

6 Click on the **Picture** button.

▶ The Picture dialog box appears. The first step is to replace the deleted hyperlink with the picture that will form the basis for the graphic hyperlink.

| 7 | Click on the **Browse** button. | |

| ▶ | The Insert Picture dialog box appears, with the contents of the My Documents folder visible. |  |

| 8 | Double-click on the file **gohome.gif.** |

▶ The Insert Picture dialog box disappears, and the Picture dialog box becomes visible again, with *gohome.gif* in the Image Source field.

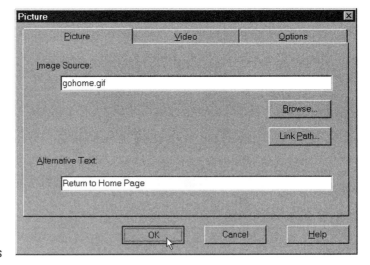

▶ Now for the alternative text. It is doubly important to include alternative text for a graphic hyperlink since the hyperlink is active even if the picture itself isn't visible. Unless you include alternative text, your text-only readers won't know where the hyperlink leads.

| 9 | In the Alternative Text field, type **Return to Home Page.** |

| 10 | Click on the **OK** button. |

▶ The Picture dialog box disappears, and the picture *gohome.gif* appears in the menu bar.

 | About Marvin's | Catalog of Wares | Write to Marvin

11 Now we need to transform the picture into a graphic hyperlink that leads to the home page. Click on the picture to select it.

 About Marvin's | Catalog of Wares | Write to Marvin

12 Click on the **Hyperlink** button.

▶ The Hyperlink dialog box appears. From here, you specify the destination of the graphic hyperlink.

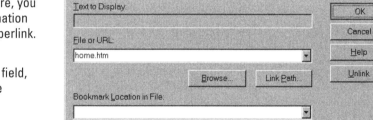

13 In the File or URL field, type the file name **home.htm.**

14 Click on the **OK** button.

▶ The Hyperlink dialog box disappears, and the picture is surrounded by a blue border, which lets you know that it is a graphic hyperlink.

 | About Marvin's | Catalog of Wares | Write to Marvin

Just for fun, let's test it out.

15 Double-click on the graphic hyperlink.

▶ The home page appears.

Marvin's Magic Shoppe

▶ ▶ ▶ **I**f you decide to use a graphic hyperlink, be sure that the picture clearly indicates where it leads. If your picture requires interpretation, you may want to include a word or two of description within the picture itself. In our example, the graphic hyperlink includes the word *Home* so that readers know that when they click on it, it will take them to the home page.

Picture Options

Internet Assistant lets you control certain aspects of the appearance and function of graphics in your Web pages. The Picture dialog box contains an Options section that allows you to:

- Adjust the dimensions of a picture
- Set the alignment of a picture alongside text in the same line
- Give pictures a border of adjustable width
- Define pictures as imagemaps

Setting Picture Dimensions

Internet Assistant allows you to specify the height and width of a picture as it's displayed when viewed with a Web browser. By doing so, you don't affect the size of the graphic file itself, just how it appears on the screen as part of a Web page.

This has important ramifications for you as a Web publisher. Remember one of the golden rules of picture usage in Web pages: that small pictures load faster than large ones? Well, "small" and "large" refer to the size of the file (in bytes), *not* the dimensions of the picture as it's displayed. This means that you can take a relatively small picture and "inflate" it by giving it larger height and width specifications, without affecting its file size. You'll still have the advantage of a fast-loading graphic, with the splash of a large, colorful picture in your Web page. In the example below, *smiley.gif* appears displayed in two sizes in Internet Explorer.

The original dimensions of the graphic are 15 pixels high and 15 pixels wide. The first smiley is displayed in the original size, while the second is twice as large (its dimensions were set with a height of 30 pixels and a width of 30 pixels). Even though the second smiley is twice as big, it downloads in the same amount of time as the first smiley, because the file size is identical.

The drawback to inflating the size of a graphic is a loss in image quality (see how the larger smiley is a bit jagged?). For that reason, use the dimension specifications sparingly, and keep the inflation ratio to a maximum of one-and-a-half times the size of the original graphic.

Changes in picture dimensions are an extension to HTML and are not visible in all Web browsers, including Internet Assistant's Web Browse view.

Another big advantage to setting picture size is that it allows your reader's Web browser to display the text *while* it is downloading the graphics. This way, readers can begin to read the contents of your page without having to wait for the entire page, complete with graphics, to appear. This may seem like a trivial detail, but it's yet another way to take your readers' perspectives into account while designing your Web pages.

  To find out the original dimensions of a picture, open the file in a graphics program (visit the Online Resource for links to some good ones). Most graphics programs include an option that allows you to see the dimensions of the graphic in pixels.

Let's set the dimensions of Marvin's logo. We'll use its original dimensions, since that is the size we'd like it to appear in the home page.

1. On the home page, click on Marvin's logo.

2. Click on the **Picture** button.

▶ The Picture dialog box appears.

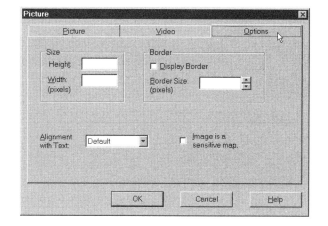

3 Click on the **Options** tab at the top of the dialog box to make that section visible.

4 In the Size section, click on the Height field and type **193**.

5 Press the **Tab** key to move the cursor to the Width field, and type **195**.

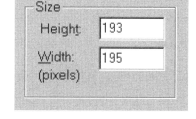

6 Click on the **OK** button.

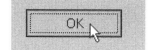

▶ There is a momentary pause while Internet Assistant inserts size specifications into your document's HTML source. The Picture dialog box disappears, and the home page becomes visible again.

7 On your own, specify the dimensions of the graphic hyperlink in the menu bar of the About Marvin's page (*gohome.gif*). Follow the same instructions as above, using the dimensions 93 for height and 75 for width.

Setting Picture Alignment with Text

Sometimes, you will want graphics in your Web pages to appear next to text on the same line or in the same paragraph. The options in this drop-down list allow you to control the vertical and horizontal position of your inline image relative to any text that is in the same line.

The following example illustrates differences in picture alignment relative to text when viewed with Internet Explorer:

☺ In this case, Smiley is aligned with the middle of the text in the line (called AbsMiddle).

Here, Smiley is aligned to the right of the text, with the rest ☺ of the line wrapping around the image (called Right).

The following table describes the functions of all of the Alignment with Text options. You'll find the same information in the Internet Assistant Help system, but I've reproduced it here for your reference.

ALIGNMENT OPTION	DESCRIPTION
Default	Aligns your inline graphic with surrounding text based on the default position determined by your reader's browser.
Left	Defines your inline graphic as a "floating" image type. The image "floats" over to the first available space at the left-hand margin. Subsequent text wraps around it to the right.
Right	Also defines your inline graphic as a "floating" image type. The image "floats" over to the first available space at the right-hand margin. Subsequent text wraps around the left-hand side of the image.
Top	Aligns your inline graphic with the top of the tallest item in the line. If the tallest item is another graphic, the top of your image will be aligned with the top of it.
TextTop	Aligns your inline graphic with the top of the tallest text in the line.
Middle	Aligns the middle of your inline graphic with the baseline of the text in the line.
AbsMiddle	Aligns the middle of your inline graphic with the middle of the text in the line; that is, the graphic and text are visually aligned at the middle of each.
Baseline and Bottom	Aligns the bottom of your inline graphic with the baseline of the text in the line.
AbsBottom	Aligns the bottom of your inline graphic with the bottom of the text in the line; that is, the graphic and text are visually aligned at the bottom of each.

  ▶ ▶ ▶ Changes in picture alignment are an extension to HTML and are not visible in all browsers, including Internet Assistant's Web Browse view.

To change picture alignment:

1 Click on the picture itself to select it.

2 Click on the **Picture** button.

▶ The Picture dialog box appears.

3 Click on the **Options** tab at the top of the dialog box.

4 Click on the down-arrow on the right side of the Alignment with Text field and select the option of your choice.

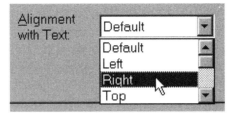

5 Click on the **OK** button.

 ▶ ▶ ▶ The Border picture option allows you to display your pictures with a black border of adjustable width. As of this writing, however, only the Netscape Navigator Web browser recognizes this tag and displays automatic borders. For that reason, I recommend using a graphics program to add a border to the image itself rather than using this function.

Inserting an Imagemap

Imagemaps, or *ISMAP graphics,* are special types of pictures that have more than one hyperlink embedded in them. Depending on where you click inside the picture, you activate a different hyperlink.

As you might expect, including imagemaps in your Web pages is more complicated than adding regular graphics. Imagemaps are made up of two distinct files: the *map* file, a text file which defines the hyperlinks associated with specific areas of the graphic, and the actual *graphic* to which it refers. While Internet Assistant knows how to display the imagemap graphic, it doesn't know how to create the map file.

To create the map file, you need to use special software. Like most Web publishing tools, map creation software is available for free over the Internet (visit the Online Resource for my picks). Once you've created a map file, you need to coordinate with your Internet service provider to activate it. Only then will the imagemap graphic in your page work properly.

  Each Internet service provider has its own process for working with map files. If you intend to include imagemaps in your website, first talk to your provider about the best way to proceed.

So, let's say you've already created your map file and your Internet service provider has activated it. You are now ready to insert the imagemap graphic into your home page. To do so, follow the same steps you did to insert a regular graphic, and in the Options section of the Picture dialog box, check the Image is a sensitive map option.

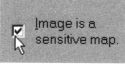

  You may have noticed another option in the Insert Picture dialog box: the Video option. This section allows you to insert inline videos into your Web pages. I'll talk about inline videos in Lesson 9.

Great job! You've covered a lot of ground in this lesson. From here, let's take a break.

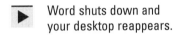 Select **File** ➢ **Exit** and respond to the dialog boxes to save your files as HTML documents. (If you feel like moving on to the next lesson right now, you can skip this step; instead, select File ➢ Save All to save the changes you've made to your files.)

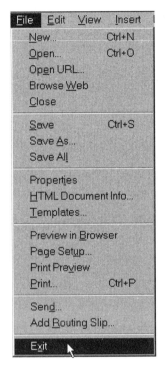

▶ Word shuts down and your desktop reappears.

In this lesson, you've snazzed up your home page with pictures and graphic hyperlinks. In the next lesson, we'll experiment with new layout possibilities by creating an HTML table.

ORGANIZING INFORMATION WITH TABLES

If you've ever used a spreadsheet or a Word table before, you know that certain types of information—schedules or price lists, for example—are easier to understand when they are presented as a table. The information is divided into categories and placed in individual *cells,* and the cells are organized by rows and columns. The good news is that you can use HTML to create tables in your Web pages. The great news is that Internet Assistant makes it a snap.

Tables give the creative Web publisher an extra bonus: they provide an amazing degree of page layout flexibility. Whereas basic HTML text layout is the traditional, one-paragraph-after-another format (with the occasional list thrown in for variety), *invisible tables* allow you to arrange text and graphics in an infinite variety of layouts. An invisible table is simply a regular table without defined borders, and it can be used as a framework for the placement of text and graphics on a page.

Here's what a traditional table looks like in Internet Explorer:

Day	*Special Flavor*
Monday	Bubble Gum
Tuesday	Pecan Praline
Wednesday	Mint Chip

Here's how an invisible table can be used as a page layout tool:

Berton's Ice cream offers premium, homemade ice cream with all of your favorite toppings. The perfect way to end a fine meal.

Conveniently located within walking distance of local theater!

Each graphic and section of text illustrated above is contained within its own invisible table cell.

▶ ▶ ▶ **W**hile most Web browsers know how to display tables, some don't. This is something to keep in mind as you design your Web pages. Some Web publishers want the majority of their readers to enjoy creative layout, and accept the consequence that the minority won't be able to read their pages. Others create a separate set of Web pages without tables for those readers using browsers that can't display them. The choice is yours.

▶ ▶ ▶ **I**n this lesson, we'll be using the Preview in Browser command to display changes in a table as we work on it. As I mentioned in Lesson 4, this feature allows you to view aspects of your HTML document that Internet Assistant doesn't know how to display. While the Preview in Browser command works with any Web browser installed on your computer, some of the features we'll be using are only visible in Internet Explorer. Internet Explorer is available for free download at Microsoft's website. If you don't already have it, I recommend downloading and installing it now. You'll find a link to Internet Explorer in the Online Resource. Once there, you'll find easy instructions for installing it on your computer.

Now that you know what tables can do, let's add one to *catalog.htm.* We'll create a table that displays the weekly schedule of Marvin's free magic workshops.

Creating a Table

The first step is to create a basic table.

1 Open Word by clicking on the **Start** button and selecting **Microsoft Word.**

▶ Word opens and presents you with a blank document.

2 Select **File ≻ Open.**

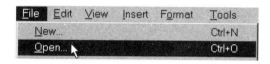

▶ The Open dialog box appears and displays the contents of your My Documents folder.

3 Double-click on **catalog.htm.**

▶ The Catalog of Wares page opens.

4 Scroll to the bottom of the document.

5 Place the cursor directly after the word **trick.**

• The Disappearing Jack: amaze your friends with this classic trick| ⌶

6 Press the ⏎ key to create a new line.

- The Disappearing Jack: amaze your friends with this classic trick
- |

7 Using the Style box, select **Heading 3, H3**.

List Bullet,UL   Á

¶ Heading 1,H1
¶ Heading 2,H2
Heading 3,H3
¶ Heading 4,H4
¶ Heading 5,H5
¶ Heading 6,H6
¶ Horizontal Rule,HR

▶ The Styles list disappears, and the line is now formatted with the Heading 3 style.

8 Type **Marvin's Free Magic Workshops**.

Marvin's Free Magic Workshops
|

9 Press the ⏎ key to create a new line where we will insert the table.

10 In the Standard toolbar, click on the **Insert Table** button.

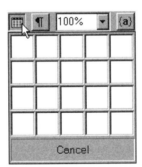

▶ A grid of white boxes appears that allows you to choose how many rows and columns you'd like your table to contain. (If you prefer to define your table using numbers of rows and columns, select Table ➤ Insert Table and type in the number of rows and columns you'd like your table to contain.)

11 Click on the third cell of the final row in the grid to define a table that's 4 rows by 3 columns.

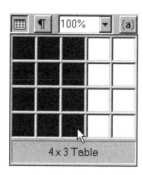

4 x 3 Table

▶ A table appears in your document.

Marvin's Free Magic Workshops

Now let's add text to the table.

1 Click on the first cell in the table and type **Day.**

Day	Time	

2 Press the **Tab** key to advance to the next cell (or click on the next cell with your cursor), and type **Time.**

3 Press the **Tab** key three times to advance to the second cell in the second row, and type **Beginning Magic.**

Day	Time	
	Beginning Magic	Advanced Tricks

4 Press **Tab** and type **Advanced Tricks.**

5 Now fill in the rest of the table as shown, pressing Tab or using the mouse to move to the next cell each time.

Marvin's Free Magic Workshops

Day	Time	
	Beginning Magic	Advanced Tricks
Monday	12-1 PM	1-2 PM
Wednesday	6-7 PM	7-8 PM

Now that we have created a basic table, let's see what it looks like. We'll use the Preview in Browser command to view the table in Internet Explorer.

1 In the Standard toolbar, click on the **Save** button (or select **File ➢ Save**).

▶ Word saves the changes you've made to *catalog.htm*.

2 Click on the **Preview in Browser** button.

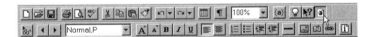

▶ There is a pause as Internet Explorer opens, and momentarily the Catalog of Wares page appears in a new viewing window.

3 Scroll down until the table is visible.

Marvin's Free Magic Workshops

Day	Time	
	Beginning Magic	Advanced Tricks
Monday	12-1 PM	1-2 PM
Wednesday	6-7 PM	7-8 PM

Adding Table Borders

As you can see, the text is arranged in a pattern of rows and columns, but the table itself is invisible. This is because we haven't yet given it borders. Internet Assistant allows you to give your tables borders of variable width and color.

 ▶ ▶ ▶ **T**able borders of variable width and color are extensions to HTML, and they won't be visible in all Web browsers. Table border color is an extension specific to the Internet Explorer browser. When viewed in other browsers, table borders appear black.

1 Click on the **Microsoft Word** button in the Taskbar to return to the Internet Assistant viewing window.

2 Select **Table ➤ Borders.**

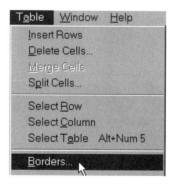

▶ The Borders dialog box appears. Here, you select whether or not you'd like your table to have borders and, if so, what their width and color will be.

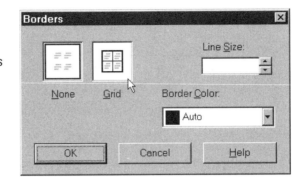

3 To specify table borders, click on the **Grid** option.

▶ The Grid option is high-lighted, and a 1 appears in the Line Size field. The Line Size field allows you to give table borders a width from 1 to 6 pixels. We'll leave this field alone, since the default value of a 1-pixel-wide border is just right for our table. The Color field allows you to choose the table border color from a drop-down list of options. We'll also leave this field unchanged, since the default value Auto creates borders that are the same color as the document's background (which is what we want).

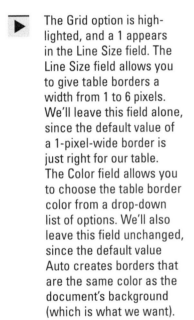

4 Click on the **OK** button.

▶ The Borders dialog box disappears, and the table borders in the document turn from dotted to solid. Let's view the change in Internet Explorer.

Marvin's Free Magic Workshops*

Day	Time	
	Beginning Magic	Advanced Tricks
Monday	12-1 PM	1-2 PM
Wednesday	6-7 PM	7-8 PM

5 Click on the **Save** button.

6 Click on the **Internet Explorer** button in the Taskbar to move to its viewing window.

▶ The table becomes visible, complete with borders.

Marvin's Free Magic Workshops		
Day	Time	
	Beginning Magic	Advanced Tricks
Monday	12-1 PM	1-2 PM
Wednesday	6-7 PM	7-8 PM

▶ ▶ ▶ **A**s we work on the table in Internet Assistant's HTML Edit view, you'll notice the appearance of blue, underlined asterisks around and within the table. These asterisks indicate special table formatting and should be left alone.

Setting the Width and Spacing of Table Columns

Internet Assistant gives you several ways to define the width of the columns in a table. You can give each column precise measurements, or you can allow your readers' browsers to determine the width of the table.

1 Click on the **Microsoft Word** button in the Taskbar to return to the Internet Assistant viewing window.

2 Select **Table** ➤ **Cell Width and Spacing**.

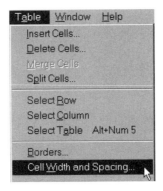

The Cell Width and Spacing dialog box appears. The WYSIWYG Column Widths check box, when checked, specifies fixed column widths that will be identical to what you see on your screen (hence the term *WYSIWYG:* "what you see is what you get"). The Cell Width section allows you to specify how you would like column width to be determined. The Automatically sized radio button, when marked, allows your reader's browser to determine the width of columns (if you'd like automatically sized columns, make sure the WYSIWYG Column Widths check box is unmarked as well). The Provide hints radio button, when marked, allows you to fix the width of columns in inches. Finally, the Cell Spacing section allows you to determine the amount of space, or *padding,* between cells.

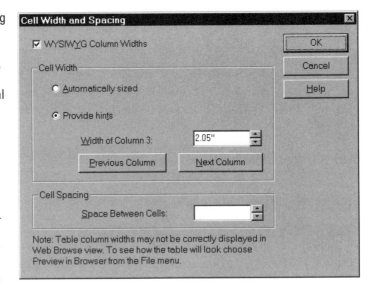

3 Let's fix the column widths of our table. Highlight the contents of the Width of Column 3 field and type **1.5"**. (Column 3 is specified here because that's where the cursor was when we selected Table ➤ Cell Width and Spacing.)

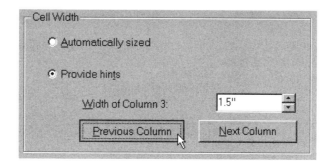

4 Click on the **Previous Column** button.

▶ The Cell Width and Spacing dialog box disappears, and there is a pause as Internet Assistant adjusts the column width. After a moment, the dialog box reappears, allowing you to set the widths of the other columns in the table.

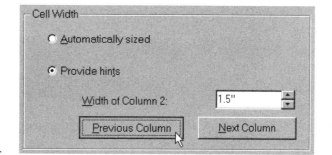

5 Type **1.5"** in the Width of Column 2 field and click on the **Previous Column** button.

6 Type **1.5** in the Width of Column 1 field and click on the **OK** button.

► The Cell Width and Spacing dialog box disappears, and the table becomes visible again, now with column widths of 1.5 inches each. Let's view the change in Internet Explorer.

Day	Time	
	Beginning Magic	Advanced Tricks
Monday	12-1 PM	1-2 PM
Wednesday	6-7 PM	7-8 PM

7 Click on the **Save** button.

8 Click on the **Internet Explorer** button in the Taskbar to move to its viewing window.

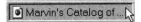

► The table, with newly sized columns, becomes visible.

Day	Time	
	Beginning Magic	Advanced Tricks
Monday	12-1 PM	1-2 PM
Wednesday	6-7 PM	7-8 PM

► ► ► **A** quick way to set the fixed width of table columns in Internet Assistant HTML Edit view is to move your cursor over a table border until it changes into a small, thick vertical line with tiny arrows on either side. You can then click on the border and drag it to the desired width.

Creating Table Headers

Traditionally, category headings in tables are distinguished from regular table text with special formatting. Internet Assistant allows you to do this easily.

1 Click on the **Microsoft Word** button in the Taskbar to return to the Internet Assistant viewing window.

2 Highlight the first two cells in the first row of the table by clicking on the first cell, holding down the mouse button, dragging the cursor over the second cell, and releasing the mouse button.

Day	Time	

3 Select **Table ➤ Cell Type.**

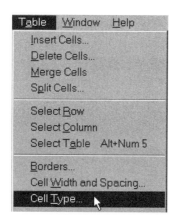

▶ The Cell Type dialog box appears.

4 Click on the **Table Header** radio button.

5 Click on the **OK** button.

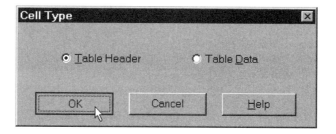

▶ The dialog box disappears, and the text in the cells becomes bold and centered (the standard format for table headers). Also, asterisks appear next to the text indicating that it has special formatting.

 ▶ ▶ ▶ **U**sing the Cell Type command to differentiate headers from regular table cells isn't mandatory; you can instead use any of the text formatting effects you learned about in Lesson 4.

Setting Table Alignment

Internet Assistant allows you to control the horizontal and vertical alignment of text within each table cell, as well as the alignment of the entire table within the body of the document.

1 Highlight the last three rows of the table.

*Day	*Time	
	Beginning Magic	Advanced Tricks
Monday	12-1 PM	1-2 PM
Wednesday	6-7 PM	7-8 PM

2   Select **Table** ➢ **Align.**

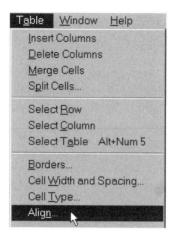

▶   The Align dialog box appears. The Entire Table section allows you to control the alignment of the table in the document: either left-aligned or centered. The default value is Left, and since this is what we want for our table, we'll leave this section alone. The Text in Table Cells section allows you to control the horizontal and vertical alignment of text within the cells.

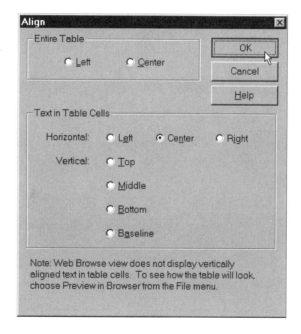

3 In the Horizontal option, click on the **Center** radio button. (The default vertical alignment is Middle, which is what we want, so we'll also leave that section alone.)

4 Click on the **OK** button.

▶ The dialog box disappears, and the selected text is centered within each cell. Also, asterisks appear next to the text indicating special formatting. Let's view the changes we've made in Internet Explorer.

*Day	*Time	
	Beginning Magic	Advanced Tricks
Monday	12-1 PM	1-2 PM
Wednesday	6-7 PM	7-8 PM

5 Click on the **Save** button.

6 Click on the **Internet Explorer** button in the Taskbar.

Marvin's Catalog of ...

▶ The table appears, with bold and centered headers and centered regular text.

Day	Time	
	Beginning Magic	Advanced Tricks
Monday	12-1 PM	1-2 PM
Wednesday	6-7 PM	7-8 PM

▶ ▶ ▶ The Table ➢ Align command is the *only* way to set the alignment of an HTML table. If you attempt to use the paragraph alignment buttons in the Formatting toolbar to align any aspect of a table, they won't work.

Merging Table Cells

Internet Assistant allows you to merge more than one cell together to form a single cell. In our case, the header Time, even though it sits above the second column, actually applies to the information in both the second and third columns. We will therefore merge the two cells above the second and third columns, so that the Time header covers both of them.

1   Click on the **Microsoft Word** button in the Taskbar to return to the Internet Assistant viewing window.

2   Highlight the second and third cells in the first row.

3   Select **Table** ➢ **Merge Cells.**

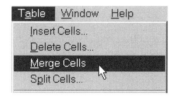

▶   The cells merge and, as a result, the second cell contains an extra space.

4   Click on the cell, placing your cursor underneath the word **Time.**

5 Press the **Backspace** key on your keyboard to delete the space.

_Day	_Time	
_*_	*Beginning Magic	*Advanced Tricks
*Monday	*12-1 PM	*1-2 PM
*Wednesday	*6-7 PM	*7-8 PM

▶ The Time header now covers both the second and third columns. Let's see how the table looks in Internet Explorer.

6 Click on the **Save** button.

7 Click on the **Internet Explorer** button in the Taskbar.

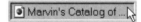

▶ The table appears. The Time header clearly applies to both columns.

Day	Time	
	Beginning Magic	Advanced Tricks
Monday	12-1 PM	1-2 PM
Wednesday	6-7 PM	7-8 PM

 ▶ ▶ ▶ **Y**ou can also split cells by highlighting a cell (or cells) and selecting Table ➤ Split Cells. When the Split Cells dialog box appears, specify the number of cells you'd like.

Adding Table Background Color

Our table is shaping up nicely. Time to brighten it up with some color. Internet Assistant allows you to add background color to table cells.

► ► ► **T**able background color is an extension to HTML specific to the Internet Explorer browser. When viewed in other browsers, table background color changes won't be visible.

1 Click on the **Microsoft Word** button in the Taskbar to return to the Internet Assistant viewing window.

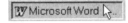

2 Highlight the first row in the table.

3 Select **Table** ➤ **Background Color.**

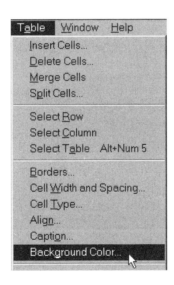

▶ The Background Color dialog box appears. Here, you specify the color you want and whether you'd like color changes to apply to specific cells or to the entire table.

4 In the Apply to option, click on the **Selected Cells** radio button.

5 Click on the down-arrow to the right of the Background Color field to display a drop-down list of choices.

6 Select **Red.**

7 Click on the **OK** button.

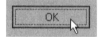

▶ The dialog box disappears, and the highlighted cells turn red (the color looks different since the cells are still highlighted).

8 Highlight the second and third cells in the second row.

9 Select **Table** ➤
Background Color.

10 In the Apply to option,
click on the **Selected
Cells** radio button.

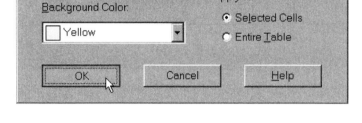

11 In the Background Color
field, select **Yellow.**

12 Click on the **OK** button.

▶ The dialog box disappears,
and the highlighted cells
turn yellow. Let's view the
color changes in Internet
Explorer.

13 Click on the **Save** button.

14 Click on the **Internet
Explorer** button in the
Taskbar.

▶ The table appears,
complete with its
colorful cells. (It's hard
to distinguish the yellow
cells from the gray in
this black-and-white
book, but you'll see all
the colors on-screen.)

These cells are red...

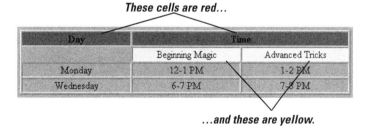

...and these are yellow.

Varying the Look of Table Text

As a finishing touch, let's apply some text formatting to the table.

1 Click on the **Microsoft Word** button in the Taskbar to return to the Internet Assistant viewing window.

2 Highlight the second and third cells in the second row.

3 In the Formatting toolbar, click on the **Italic** button.

▶ The highlighted text becomes italicized.

4 Highlight the first row.

5 Select **Format** ➤ **Font**.

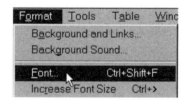

▶ The Font dialog box appears.

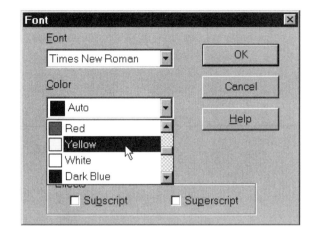

6   Click on the down-arrow to the right of the Color field and select **Yellow** from the drop-down list that appears.

7   Click on the **OK** button.

▶ The dialog box disappears and the highlighted text turns yellow. Let's view our finished table in Internet Explorer.

8   Click on the **Save** button.

9   Click on the **Internet Explorer** button in the Taskbar.

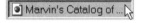

▶ Congratulations—you've just created a beautiful table!

Marvin's Free Magic Workshops

Day	Time	
	Beginning Magic	*Advanced Tricks*
Monday	12-1 PM	1-2 PM
Wednesday	6-7 PM	7-8 PM

► ► ► The Table command also contains an option that allows you to add a caption either above or below your table (Table ➤ Caption). In our example, we created a table title at the beginning of the lesson, so a caption is unnecessary.

You've done a great job. Time for a break.

1 Select **File** ➤ **Exit** and respond to the dialog boxes to save your file as an HTML document. (If you feel like moving on to the next lesson right now, you can skip this step and select File ➤ Save All to save the changes you've made to your file.)

► Word closes and your desktop reappears.

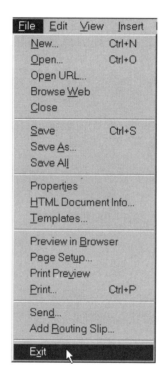

In the next lesson, we'll make it easy for your readers to send you feedback by creating an interactive form.

Making Your Web Pages Interactive with Forms

The Web's colorful, information-packed, surfable quality makes it the perfect place to tell the world about yourself (or your company or cause). When you put up a website, you erect an electronic billboard of sorts, there for all to see. While this is a powerful method of communication, it's passive; all your website can do is be seen. Imagine your readers as commuters zooming along on the freeway (I'll resist the information superhighway metaphor here). They see your billboard, and many may take a closer look, but then they're off, speeding along to their next destination.

In this lesson, we'll add a new dimension to your website: interactivity. We'll let your readers do more than just look at your site; we'll give them a way to send instant feedback right to your e-mailbox. How? By creating an *interactive form.*

Interactive forms are very much like regular paper forms. They collect different types of data by prompting readers to fill in *fields,* either by typing information or by selecting an item in a list. Once your readers have completed the form, they click on a button (usually at the bottom of the page) that transmits the information to the website's administrator.

You can use forms in your Web pages for many different purposes: to survey visitors to your site, to solicit requests for further information, or to invite feedback, just to name a few. In this lesson, we'll create a simple feedback form that will find out some basic information about Marvin's visitors and will allow them to send in their questions and comments.

How Forms Work

Before we begin, allow me give you a quick-and-dirty introduction to interactive forms. I'll dispense with the technical details since the goal here is to give you a general idea of what happens when a form is filled out and submitted.

As I mentioned earlier, interactive forms consist of one or more fields. Fields are the places your readers fill in the information you request. There are three types of fields you can include in an HTML form:

- Fields in which readers enter any information they wish
- Fields in which readers select from a list of predefined choices
- Hidden fields that are invisible to the reader but that include data of your choosing along with the information they submit (I'll explain why this is useful later in this lesson)

You can include as many fields of as many types as you like in your form.

Here is an example of a simple form that contains two fields: one, a field for the reader's name, and the other, a selection list that allows them to choose their favorite color.

My name is Asha, and my favorite color is Chartreuse ±

> Chartreuse
> **Magenta**
> Violet
> Scarlet

Submit

Once the form is complete, the reader clicks on the *Submit* button. This button activates the reader's browser to send the information contained in the form to the Web server on which the website is located. This is how the information looks when it is sent to the Web server:

Field names

`Name=Asha&Color=Magenta`

Field values

The information is compiled into a list of *name/value pairs.* The *name* is a label you assign to each field in your form. The *value* is the information submitted by the reader.

The final step is for the Web server to put this line of text into some readable format and send it to the website's administrator (i.e., you) via e-mail. This is not automatic; it requires coordination with your Internet service provider. Your provider must write and activate a special program called a *CGI script* to process form submissions.

  Some Internet service providers create "generic" form-processing CGI scripts that can be used by all of their customers. Other providers charge a fee to write custom CGI scripts for those users who need them. Find out your provider's policy before you include forms in your website.

Once the forms-processing script is in place, it does two things:

- It formats the information it receives each time a reader submits a form.
- It bounces the formatted information to you via e-mail.

So, instead of receiving a weird-looking line of text and codes (like the one on the previous page), you get a well-organized list of field names followed by their values.

There is a way around the scripting issue. Some Web browsers allow you to submit form information *directly* to an e-mail address—bypassing the Web server and CGI script altogether. Of course, the information will look like the hodgepodge of text in the above illustration, but if it's a short form with only a few fields, that might be okay for you.

  Internet Assistant's Web Browse view doesn't know how to process form information sent directly to an e-mail address. In other words, if you are browsing the Web using Internet Assistant and you come upon a form that is programmed to submit its data to an e-mail address, you won't be able to use it. You can, however, use Internet Assistant to *create* a form that sends information directly to an e-mail address.

Now that you have a sense of how forms work, let's add one to Marvin's website. The CD included with the book contains an HTML file called *write.htm*. We'll use it as the basis for a feedback form.

  Before you begin this lesson, copy *write.htm* from the CD to the My Documents folder on your hard drive.

Creating a Form

write.htm is no different than any other Web page at this point—I've only included it here in order to save you from doing a bunch of typing.

1 Open Word by clicking on the **Start** button and selecting **Microsoft Word.**

▶ Word opens and presents you with a blank document.

2 Select **File ➣ Open.**

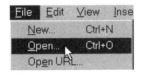

▶ The Open dialog box appears and displays the contents of your My Documents folder.

3 Double-click on **write.htm.**

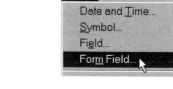

▶ *write.htm* opens.

4 Place the cursor to the
right of the word *Name:*
(leave a space after the
colon).

Tell Marvin What You Think

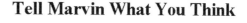

Marvin is happy to answer questions about his shop or his products. He would also love to hea
website. Use this form to tell Marvin what you think.

Name: | I

E-mail address (so Marvin can write back to you):

5 Select **Insert** ➢
Form Field.

▶ The New Form dialog box
appears, letting you know
that you are adding a form
to your HTML document.

6 Click on the **Continue**
button.

▶ Form attributes appear
in your document.

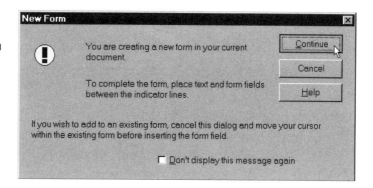

Let's pause to take a look around. Three things have just changed in your document,
as shown in the illustration on the next page: first, lines have appeared that define where
the form begins and ends. These *form boundaries* demarcate a special section within the
Web page where you can insert form fields. As you can see, a form isn't a *separate* document, but a specific type of HTML *within* a document. Second, a new toolbar has appeared:
the *Forms toolbar.* Here, you have at your disposal all of the tools required to create and
edit an HTML form. Finally, the *Form Field dialog box* has appeared. This dialog box allows
you to choose the type of field you'd like to add to your form. I'll explain what each field
type is as we go along.

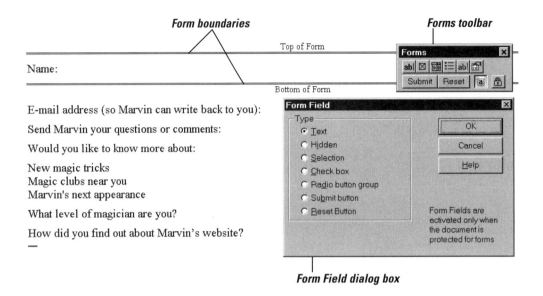

Form boundaries

Forms toolbar

Form Field dialog box

► ► ► If you prefer using toolbars in the conventional, at-the-top-of-the-document view (that is, an *anchored* toolbar as opposed to a *floating* one), double-click anywhere on the blank area of the Forms toolbar.

Adding Form Fields

Form fields are the receptacles that collect information from your readers. The type of fields you use in your form depend on the type of information you want to gather. Do you want your readers to select an option from a list of choices you define? Do you want them to fill in the blank? The answers to these questions will tell you which field is appropriate in each case.

As you add fields to your form, you customize them by giving each one a name, in some cases a value, and any special formatting you like.

Text Fields

The most basic type of form field is called a *text field.* Your readers may enter any data they wish into a text field. This is useful when you want to collect information that's different for each person (such as a name or comments). Let's add some text fields to your document and customize them so they look like and do exactly what we want.

1 In the Form Field dialog box, click on the **OK** button.

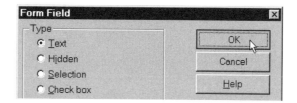

▶ The Text Form Field dialog box appears. This dialog box allows you to customize the field you just created. The most important step is to give the field a name.

2 Click on the Name field and type **Name.**

3 Click on the **OK** button.

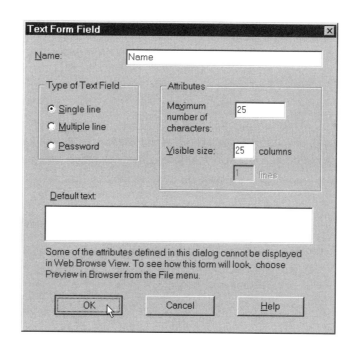

The Text Form Field dialog box disappears, and a gray box appears next to the word *Name:*. This is the text field in which your readers will eventually type their names.

You're on your way to creating a beautiful form!

  See the button on the Forms toolbar that looks like an *a* surrounded by shading? That's the *Form Field Shading* button, and you can use it to turn field shading on and off. I recommend leaving shading on for two reasons: first, the form fields become invisible without it, and second, it has no effect on the form when it is viewed with another browser.

As you can see, Internet Assistant has only placed form boundaries around the line where you inserted your first field. So, before we can continue, we need to take a slight detour and move the rest of the text on the page inside the form boundaries.

  In this case, we began our form with the text already written. You can, of course, write the text as you create your form, thereby placing the text within the form boundaries as you go.

1 Highlight all of the body text beginning with **E-mail** and ending with **website?**.

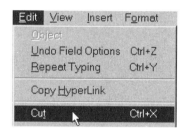

2 Select **Edit** ➢ **Cut** (or use the keyboard shortcut **Ctrl+X**).

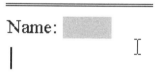

3 Place the cursor directly after the Name field.

4 Press ↵.

5 Select **Edit** ➢ **Paste** (or use the keyboard shortcut **Ctrl+V**).

▶ The text appears within the form boundaries.

Top of Form

Name:

E-mail address (so Marvin can write back to you):

Send Marvin your questions or comments:

Would you like to know more about:

New magic tricks
Magic clubs near you
Marvin's next appearance

What level of magician are you?

How did you find out about Marvin's website?

Bottom of Form

Detour over. Now we can continue.

Limiting the Maximum Number of Characters

Let's add another text field for the reader's e-mail address, so that Marvin can reply to comments and questions he receives. This time, we'll limit the length of the text that readers can enter into the field (since there aren't any e-mail addresses that are longer than 50 characters).

▶ ▶ ▶ Make a habit of placing size limits on your text fields. Generous size limits accommodate the most enthusiastic of respondents, while placing a cap on those who want to use your feedback form as a personal sounding board.

1. Place the cursor at the end of the line that reads **E-mail address (so Marvin can write back to you):** (leave a space after the colon).

E-mail address (so Marvin can write back to you):

2 In the Forms toolbar, click on the **Text Box Form Field** button (or select **Insert** ➤ **Form Field** and select the **Text** radio button).

▶ The Text Form Field dialog box appears.

3 In the Name field, type **E-mail address.**

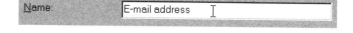

▶ The Attributes section of the dialog box allows you to control the size of the field and the maximum length of the text that can be entered there.

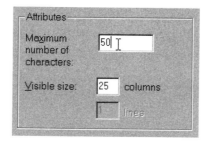

4 Double-click on the Maximum number of characters field to select it, and type **50.**

▶ The next field, Visible size, controls the size of the field itself. You may choose to keep the field size equal to the maximum length of text for that field (giving your readers a visual indication of how much space they have to type), or you may choose a different size. The size you choose will not affect the amount of text readers can enter there.

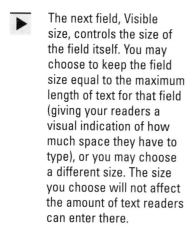

5 Press the **Tab** key to
select the contents of
the next field, and type **50**.

6 Click on the **OK** button.

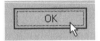

▶ The Text Form Field
dialog box disappears,
and the text form field
appears in the document
as a gray box.

E-mail address (so Marvin can write back to you):

Now if a reader tries to enter text that is longer than 50 characters into this field, he or she
will be met with a prohibitive "beep!"

  ▶ ▶ ▶ **W**hile Internet Assistant can create text fields of various sizes, the different sizes won't be apparent until you view the form using another Web browser. Internet Assistant displays all form fields as five characters long no matter what.

Creating a Multiple-Line Text Field

You can use the size of the text field as a cue to let the reader know how much information
to include. For example, if you want your readers to send you comments, giving them a big
space in which to type lets them know that you're interested in what they have to say.

Let's create a multiple-line text field to collect the comments of Marvin's visitors. We'll then
view the changes in Internet Explorer using the Preview in Browser command.

1 Place your cursor directly after the sentence **Send Marvin your questions or comments:**.

Send Marvin your questions or comments: |

▶ Since you will be creating a field that is larger than a regular field, you should put it on its own line so it has enough room.

2 Press the ↵ key.

Send Marvin your questions or comments:

|

3 In the Forms toolbar, click on the **Text Box Form Field** button.

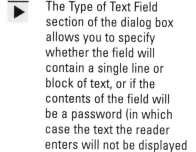

▶ The Text Form Field dialog box appears.

4 In the Name field, type **Comments.**

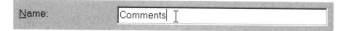

Name: [Comments]

▶ The Type of Text Field section of the dialog box allows you to specify whether the field will contain a single line or block of text, or if the contents of the field will be a password (in which case the text the reader enters will not be displayed as they type).

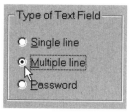

Type of Text Field

○ Single line
◉ Multiple line
○ Password

5 Click on the **Multiple line** option.

▶ The Attributes section of the dialog box allows you to define the maximum length of text input and the size of the field.

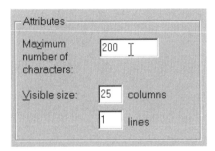

6 In the Maximum number of characters field, type **200.**

▶ Since you defined this field as having multiple lines, both the horizontal (columns) and vertical (lines) size controls in the Visible size section are active.

7 Press the **Tab** key to highlight the contents of the next field.

8 Type **40.**

9 Press the **Tab** key.

10 Type **5.**

▶ To save your readers' time and typing fingers, you can tell Internet Assistant to automatically display text in a given field. This is called *default text*. It is what appears in a field unless your readers type over it.

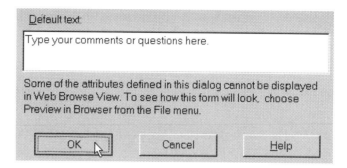

11 Click on the Default text field and type **Type your comments or questions here.**

12 Click on the **OK** button.

▶ The Text Form Field dialog box disappears, and the text field appears in the document, complete with default text.

Now, let's see what the form looks like in Internet Explorer.

13 In the Standard toolbar, click on the **Preview in Browser** button.

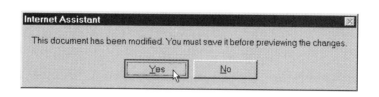

▶ The Internet Assistant dialog box appears, saying that you must save the changes to your document before previewing it in a browser.

14 Click on the **Yes** button.

There is a pause
as Internet Explorer
launches, then the
browser viewing
window appears and
displays your form.

Quite a difference, isn't it? As you can see below, the fields are of different sizes, and the comments field contains default text.

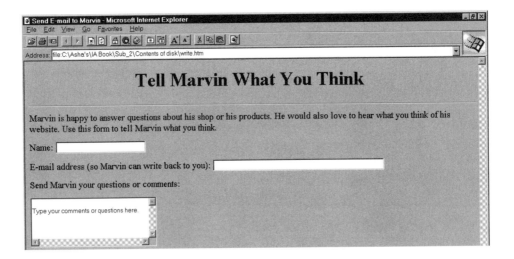

Check Box Fields

Check boxes are perfect for occasions when you want to present your readers with a short list of options from which they can choose and you would like all of the options to be visible at once. Your readers click on the check boxes to choose as many options as they like (including zero).

Let's add a list of check boxes to Marvin's home page.

1 Click on the **Microsoft Word** button in the Taskbar to return to the Internet Assistant viewing window.

2 Place the cursor directly before the word **New.**

3 In the Forms toolbar, click on the **Check Box Form Field** button.

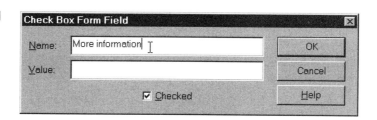

▶ The Check Box Form Field dialog box appears. Here, you can define the name and value of each field you create.

▶ Since the check boxes are being used in a group, it makes sense to give each field in the group the same name. In our case, each check box field signifies a request for more information.

4 In the Name field, type **More information.**

5 Press the **Tab** key to move the cursor to the next field.

▶ Unlike a text field, where the reader's text input is the field's value, you must define the value for check box fields. Since a check box field has only two states, marked and unmarked, you need to tell Internet Assistant what a marked field signifies. In this case, if a check box is marked, it means that the reader would like more information about that particular topic.

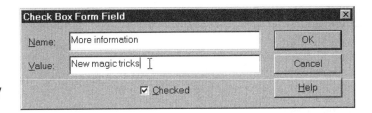

6 In the Value field, type **New magic tricks.**

▶ Finally, the Checked check box at the bottom of the dialog box allows you to choose if you would like the field to appear automatically marked.

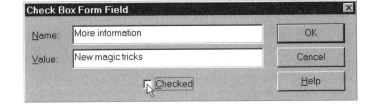

7 Click on the **Checked** check box to unmark it.

8 Click on the OK button.

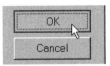

▶ The Check Box Form Field dialog box disappears, and a check box field appears in the document.

☐New magic tricks
Magic clubs near you
Marvin's next appearance

9 On your own, add check box fields to the next two lines in the list. Name each field "More information," and use the values "Magic clubs" and "Marvin's next appearance." Also, specify that each of the fields appears unmarked.

Radio Button Fields

Radio buttons are similar to check boxes in that they present your readers with a visible list of options from which to choose. The difference, however, is that readers can only make one choice (much like when you press the station buttons on your car stereo: you press one, and the one that was pressed in pops out).

1 Place the cursor after the sentence **What level of magician are you?**.

What level of magician are you? |ᴵ

2 In the Forms toolbar, click on the **Radio Button Form Field** button.

▶ The Radio Button Group Form Field dialog box appears. Instead of defining the names and values individually, as you did for check boxes, this dialog box allows you to give the entire group of fields one name, and define their values at the same time.

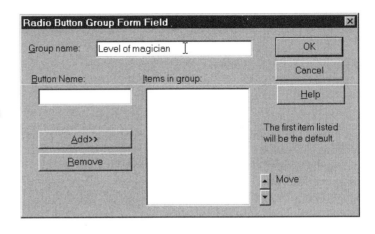

3 In the Group name field, type **Level of magician.**

▶ The items you type into the Button Name field and add to the Items in group box correspond to the values for each of the radio button fields.

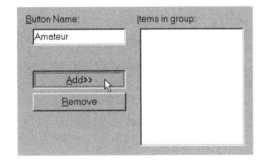

4 Click on the Button Name field and type **Amateur.**

5 Click on the **Add** button (or press the ↵ key) to add the field value to the list of items in the group.

▶ *Amateur* appears in the Items in group box. Now, let's add two more field values.

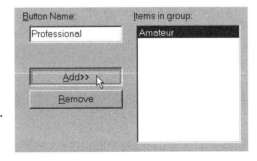

6 Click on the Button Name field and type **Professional.**

7 Click on the **Add** button.

8 Click on the Button Name field and type **Sorcerer.**

9 Click on the **Add** button.

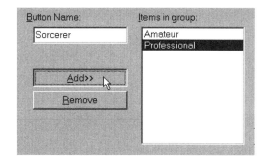

▶ The finished group of radio buttons will appear in the same order as the list in the Items in group box. If you would like to change the order of the items, you can use the Move buttons to the right of the box.

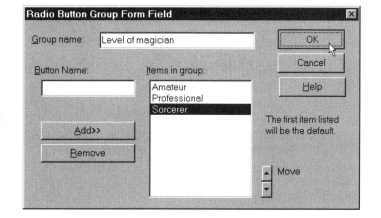

10 Click on the **OK** button.

▶ The Radio Button Group Form Field dialog box disappears, and a row of radio button fields appears in the document.

What level of magician are you? ☐Amateur ☐Professional ☐Sorcerer

In Internet Assistant, the radio button fields look just like check boxes. Let's see how they look in Internet Explorer.

11 Select **File** ➤ **Save** to save the changes we've made so far.

▶ Word saves *write.htm*.

12 Click on the **Internet Explorer** button in the Taskbar to switch to its viewing window.

▶ Your document appears. As you can see, check boxes and radio buttons look much different in Internet Explorer. Check boxes appear as little squares; when they're selected, checkmarks appear inside. Radio buttons appear as little circles; when they're selected, round buttons appear inside.

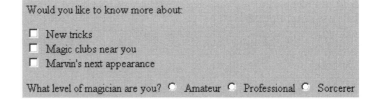

Selection List Fields

You have another option if you'd like your readers to select from a list of choices you define: you can use a *selection list* field. When a reader clicks on a selection list field (also known as a *drop-down list*), a list of choices appears, and they can select the one they want. Selection list fields are useful when you have a long list of choices and would like to save space in your document by not making the entire list visible at once.

You can create selection fields that allow your readers one or multiple choices from the list.

Single-Selection Lists

1 Click on the **Microsoft Word** button in the Taskbar to return to the Internet Assistant viewing window.

2 Place the cursor after the sentence **How did you find out about Marvin's website?**.

How did you find out about Marvin's website?

3 In the Forms toolbar, click on the **Selection List Form Field** button.

▶ The Selection Form Field dialog box appears. As with radio buttons, you give the entire group one name, and you specify the values for each item. The difference, however, is that the items as they appear on the list and their actual field values are not necessarily the same. In the Name field, you type the items as you would like them to appear in the list. In the Value when selected field, you enter values for each of the items; they may be identical or slightly different from the items themselves.

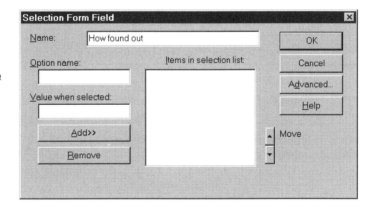

4 In the Name field, type **How found out.**

5 Click on the Option name field and type **A friend told me.**

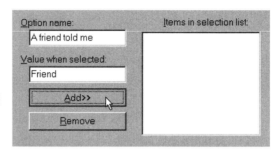

6 Press the **Tab** key to move to the Value when selected field, and type **Friend.**

7 Click on the **Add** button.

▶ The item appears to the right in the Items in selection list box. Let's add two more items.

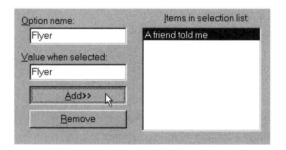

8 Click on the Option name field and type **Flyer.**

9 Press the **Tab** key to move to the Value when selected field, and type **Flyer.**

10 Click on the **Add** button.

11 Click on the Option name field and type **Websurfing.**

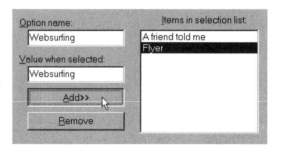

12 Press the **Tab** key to move to the Value when selected field, and type **Websurfing.**

13 Click on the **Add** button.

▶ The finished selection list will appear in the same order as the list in the Items in selection list box, with the first item in the list visible before the reader clicks on the field. If you would like to change the order of the items, you can use the Move buttons to the right of the box.

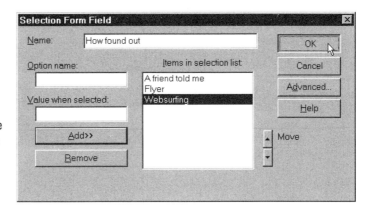

14 Click on the **OK** button.

▶ The Selection Form Field dialog box disappears, and the field appears with the first item on the list visible automatically.

How did you find out about Marvin's website? A friend told me

Let's take a peek at how your new selection list field looks in Internet Explorer.

15 Select **File ➢ Save** to save the changes to your document.

16 Click on the **Internet Explorer** button in the Taskbar to move to its viewing window.

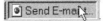

▶ Your document appears. Here is how a selection list field looks in Internet Explorer. To view the selection list, click on the down-arrow or the field itself. To select an item, move your cursor over the item to highlight it, and click. The selected item will appear in the field.

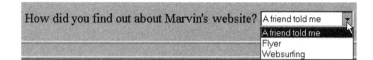

Multiple-Selection Lists

You can give your readers additional flexibility by allowing them to select more than one item from a selection list field. Let's change the field we just created into a multiple-selection list.

1 Click on the **Microsoft Word** button in the Taskbar to return to the Internet Assistant viewing window.

2 Click on the selection list field.

3 In the Forms toolbar, click on the **Field Properties** button (or double-click on the field itself).

▶ The Selection Form Field dialog box appears.

4 Click on the **Advanced** button.

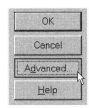

▶ The dialog box expands to reveal two options. The first check box turns the selection list field into a multiple-choice list. The second check box allows you to specify which item will be visible in the field when it's not active (remember, the default item is the first one in the list).

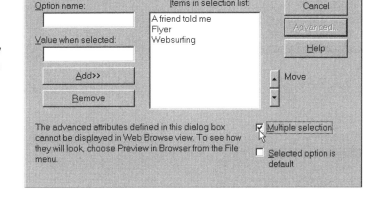

5 Click on the **Multiple selection** check box.

6 Click on the **OK** button.

▶ The Selection Form Field dialog box disappears, and the selection list field in your document has turned into what appears to be a row of radio buttons.

How did you find out about Marvin's website? ☐A friend told me ☐Flyer ☐Websurfing

Internet Assistant doesn't know how to display a multiple-selection list field. So let's view it with Internet Explorer.

7 Select **File** ➤ **Save** to save the changes to your document.

8 Click on the **Internet Explorer** button in the Taskbar to move to its viewing window.

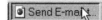

▶ Your document appears. Here is how a multiple-selection list field looks in Internet Explorer. All of the list items are visible. To select more than one item, hold down the Ctrl key while clicking on the ones you want.

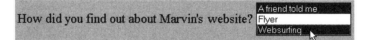

Hidden Fields

Hidden fields allow you to include "invisible" information with the data your readers send you when they submit the form. This can be helpful when you'd like to add information to the form that readers don't need to see.

For example, let's say Marvin has two websites: a professional one that showcases his magic store, and a personal one he dabbles with for fun. Both websites contain feedback forms that are submitted to the same place. To differentiate submissions from each form, Marvin can add a hidden field that identifies the source of the submission (the professional site or the personal site).

Let's try it out.

1 Click on the **Microsoft Word** button in the Taskbar to return to the Internet Assistant viewing window.

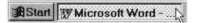

2 Place the cursor after the selection list field.

3 Press the ↵ key to insert some space between the field and the bottom of the form.

How did you find out about Marvin's website? ☐A friend told me ☐Flyer ☐Websurfing

4 Click on the **Hidden Form Field** button in the Forms toolbar.

▶ The Hidden Form Field dialog box appears. Since the information in a hidden field is static (it doesn't change), you simply specify a name and a value for the field.

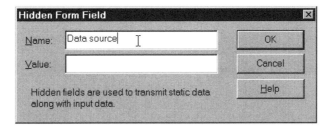

5 In the Name field, type **Data source.**

6 Click on the **Tab** key to move to the next field.

7 In the Value field, type **Professional website.** (Marvin can add a hidden field to the form in his other website with the value "Personal site" so that submissions from each form will be discernible from each other.)

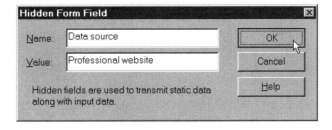

8 Click on the **OK** button.

▶ The Hidden Form Field
dialog box disappears,
and a field appears in
your document. In this
case, the blue, underlined
text does not indicate
that it is a hyperlink, but
a hidden form field.

Professional website

 ▶ ▶ ▶ The hidden form field is visible in Internet Assistant's HTML Edit view just
to remind you it's there. In Web Browse view (and in other browsers), the
field is invisible.

Congratulations! You've just completed the bulk of your form. Just one final detail…

Adding Submit and Reset Buttons

You've created a thoughtfully planned form for your readers to fill out. Now it's time to give
them a way to send you the information. Enter the *Submit button*. This elegant little tool is
the linchpin of your form, because it tells Internet Assistant what to do with the information
and where to send it.

The Submit button's partner, the *Reset button,* gives your readers an easy way to clear the
contents of the form with one click.

1 Place the cursor after
the hidden field we just
created.

Professional website |

2 Press the ⌐ key to add
some space between
the field and the bottom
of the form.

Professional website

|

3 In the Forms toolbar, click on the **Submit** button.

▶ The Submit Button Form Field dialog box appears. Here, you specify how the Submit button will look and what it will do. In the Appearance section, you specify how the button will look. If you choose Text, you will get a standard rectangular button with the text label of your choice on top. If you choose Picture, you can specify a nifty graphic (GIF or JPG, of course) to use as your button. Let's add a text button, but we'll change the staid *Submit* label into something more inviting.

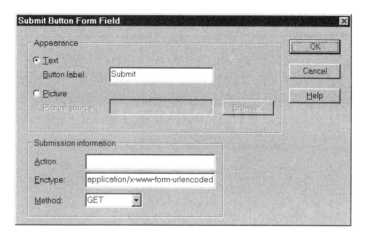

4 In the Button label field, highlight the word **Submit** (in order to type over it), and type **Send to Marvin**.

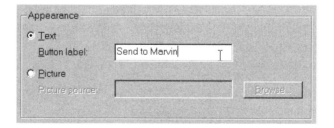

Let's stop here for a moment, since the next part of the dialog box requires some explanation. The Submission information section allows you to program the Submit button to send the form's information to the right location in the right structure. Let's go through what each of these fields does.

The *Action* field is where you enter the destination of the form contents. This destination is the URL of a Web server equipped with a CGI script that knows how to process the form data. For illustration purposes, we'll take advantage of a public script made available by the National Center of Supercomputing Applications (NCSA) at the University of Illinois. This script isn't programmed to send the form data to your e-mail; rather, it displays it nicely on your screen so you can see what formatted form data looks like.

 ▶ ▶ ▶ **W**hen it comes time for you to create a real working form, you *must* get the data sent to you via e-mail. If you've arranged with your Internet service provider to use a CGI script, you enter its URL in the Action field (your provider will tell you the correct URL). If you would rather bypass the script and have the information sent directly to your e-mailbox, you enter a faux-URL called a *mailto* in the Action field. A mailto consists of the text **mailto:** followed directly by your e-mail address. Here is what a sample mailto looks like: **mailto:marvin@magic.com**.

The *Enctype* field is where you specify the format of the form's data. You don't need to change anything in this field (Internet Assistant has taken care of the proper settings for you).

The *Method* field is where you specify how you would like Internet Assistant to submit the information. You have two choices here: POST and GET. Suffice it to say that for 99% of Web-based forms, the correct method is POST.

▶ ▶ ▶ **T**hese "explanations" are minimal at best. Unfortunately, it's difficult to say much about HTML form submission without venturing far into the wilds of techie-land. I've included the bare-bones information you need to create a workable form. If you would like to know more of the technical detail behind how HTML forms are submitted, speak with the Webmaster at your Internet service provider.

Okay. Back to the form.

5 In the Action field, enter **http://hoohoo.ncsa.uiuc. edu/htbin-post/post-query** (this is the URL of NCSA's public form script I mentioned earlier).

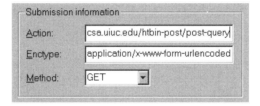

6 Click on the down-arrow of the Method field to display its drop-down list.

7 Select **POST**.

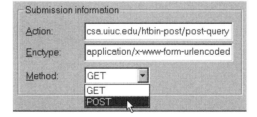

▶ POST appears in the Method field.

8 Click on the **OK** button.

▶ The Submit button (with the label "Send to Marvin") appears in your document.

Let's not forget the Submit button's partner, the Reset button.

9 Click on the **Reset** button in the Forms toolbar.

▶ The Reset Button Form Field dialog box appears. The Reset button can only be a text button, not a graphic button.

10 Highlight the contents of the Button label field and type **Start over.**

11 Click on the **OK** button.

▶ The Reset Button Form Field dialog box disappears, and the Reset button (with the label "Start over") appears in the document.

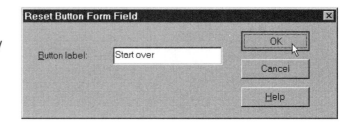

And you're done!

▶ ▶ ▶ If you would like to change the Submit button's settings after you've created it, click on it, then click on the Submit button in the Forms toolbar to display the Submit Button Field dialog box. If you double-click on the Submit button itself (as you can do to display the dialog box for every other type of form field), you will activate it, and it will attempt to begin the submission process. Don't worry—if you accidentally activate the Submit button, click on the Cancel button in the Downloading dialog box to stop it.

Protecting and Testing Your Form

Since you've put so much hard work into creating your form, you'll want to protect it from accidental changes.

1 Click on the **Protect Form** button in the Forms toolbar.

▶ When the form is protected, you're unable to make changes to it. If you find that you need to edit the form later, you can always "unprotect" it by clicking on the Protect Form button again.

Now that your form is protected, let's rev it up and see how it works! In the example, I'll use Internet Explorer to test the form and submit it. You can also switch to Internet Assistant's Web Browse view and test it from there.

▶ ▶ ▶ To test your form, you need to activate your Internet connection now.

1 Select **File** ➢ **Save** to save the changes to your document.

2 Click on the **Internet Explorer** button in the Taskbar to move to its viewing window.

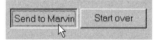

▶ Your form appears.

3 Fill out the form, entering any data and selecting anything from the selection lists you like.

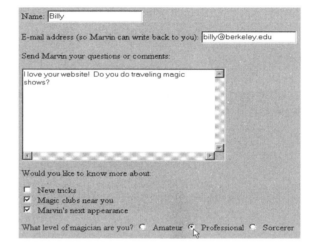

4 Click on the **Send to Marvin** button.

▶ There is a pause as the browser submits the form information, then NCSA's public CGI script returns the data, formatted and organized, to your screen. The form data is listed in order, with the field names on the left, followed by = signs, and the form values on the right.

Query Results

You submitted the following name/value pairs:

- Name = Billy
- E-mail address = billy@berkeley.edu
- Comments = I love your website! Do you do travelling magic shows?
- More information = Magic clubs
- More information = Marvin's next appearance
- Level of magician = Professional
- How found out = Flyer
- Data source = Professional website

Ah, the satisfaction of a job well done.

  ▶ ▶ ▶ **T**his form example illustrates the different types of fields, but is otherwise rather plain. Feel free to use HTML's formatting effects and graphics capabilities to spruce it up. You'll find form layout tips in the Internet Assistant Help system.

You've accomplished a lot in this lesson: time to give yourself a pat on the back and exit Word.

1   Select **File** ➤ **Exit** and respond to the dialog boxes to save write.htm as an HTML document. (If you feel like moving on to the next lesson right now, select File ➤ Save.)

▶   Word saves your document, shuts down, and your desktop reappears.

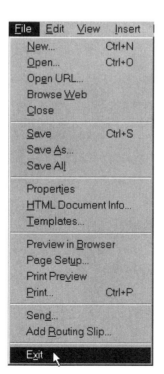

In this lesson, you've created an interactive form. In the next lesson, we'll add exciting design effects that will place your website on the cutting edge.

FANCY DESIGN EFFECTS

At this point, you're fully equipped to create a well-organized, nicely designed Web page. Armed with Internet Assistant and some Web publishing savvy, you've now got everything you need to become a true-blue Web publisher. In this lesson, I'll introduce you to some fancy design effects you can use to make your pages even snazzier.

These effects are purely optional—in fact they are more for fun than anything else—but they offer you a great way to dress up your website and express your creativity.

 ▶ ▶ ▶ **T**he flip side is that these effects won't be displayed by all browsers—including Internet Assistant's Web Browse view. In fact, certain features such as marquees, background sound, and inline video clips will appear *only* in Internet Explorer. For this reason, make sure that your site's design doesn't depend too heavily on the use of fancy effects.

 ▶ ▶ ▶ **B**efore you begin this lesson, copy *backgrnd.gif, welcome.wav,* and *marvin.avi* from the CD to the My Documents folder on your hard drive.

Changing the Background

Let's say you'd like your pages to appear with the text on a backdrop of shocking yellow or a funky, colorful image. You can do both with Internet Assistant's help.

 ▶ ▶ ▶ **B**ackground changes are an extension to HTML and won't be visible in all Web browsers.

Changing the Background Color

You can choose from a wide array of colors for the background of your document.

1 Open Word by clicking on the **Start** button and selecting **Microsoft Word.**

▶ Word opens and presents you with a blank document.

2 Select **File ➢ Open.**

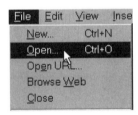

▶ The Open dialog box appears and displays the contents of your My Documents folder.

3 Double-click on **home.htm.**

▶ Marvin's home page opens.

4 Select **Format** ➢ **Background and Links.**

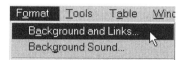

▶ The Background and Links dialog box appears. Here you can specify how you would like the background of your document to look.

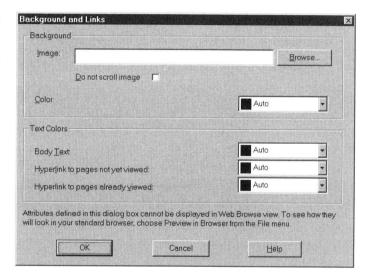

5 Click on the **Color** field to display a drop-down list of color choices.

6 Select **Yellow.**

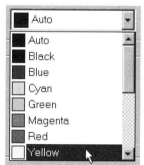

7 Click on the **OK** button.

► The Background and Links
dialog box disappears, and
the **<BODY...>** tag appears
at the top of the document.

<BODY ...>

The **<BODY...>** tag isn't a hyperlink. It's Internet Assistant's way of letting you know that
you have made a change to the HTML tag called **<BODY>** in your document. The **<BODY>**
tag is one of several standard tags Internet Assistant automatically inserts into every HTML
document you create. When you set the background color, Internet Assistant adds a
special code for that color to the **<BODY>** tag. The code, called a *hexadecimal code,* is
recognized by all Web browsers that know how to display background color. When they
encounter the hexadecimal code in the **<BODY>** tag, they translate it into its corresponding color and display it on your screen.

► ► ► There are hexadecimal codes for every color in the spectrum. While
Internet Assistant includes built-in support for the colors in its drop-down
list, you can still have access to the other colors by inserting their codes
into the **<BODY>** tag by editing the document's HTML source. You'll find a
handy reference list of hexadecimal codes and their corresponding colors,
plus instructions for inserting them into your document, in the Online
Resource.

Since Internet Assistant's Web Browse view doesn't recognize background changes, let's view the home page in Internet Explorer using the Preview in Browser command.

1 Select **File** ➤ **Save** to save the changes to the document.

2 Click on the **Preview in Browser** button.

▶ There is a pause as Internet Explorer launches, then the home page appears in the viewing window. The background of Marvin's home page is now bright yellow.

Using a Picture as the Background

If a solid color background is too conservative for you (although I would argue that bright yellow is anything but conservative!), you can use a picture as your background. Any GIF or JPG image can become the backdrop of an HTML document.

How the picture appears when displayed as a background will differ depending on the size of the image itself. The Web browser automatically *tiles* the image to create a background; in other words, it repeats the image over and over until it fills the screen, creating a uniform background for the text.

Let's replace the yellow background with an image.

1 Click on the **Microsoft Word** button in the Taskbar to return to its viewing window.

2 Select **Format ➤ Background and Links** (or double-click on the **<BODY...>** tag).

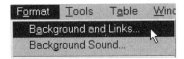

▶ The Background and Links dialog box appears.

3 In the Background section, click on the **Browse** button.

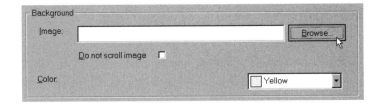

▶ The Insert Picture dialog box appears. This is the same dialog box you used to insert the logo and menu bar pictures in Lesson 6.

4 Double-click on the file name **backgrnd.gif.**

▶ The Insert Picture dialog box disappears, and the Background and Links dialog box becomes visible again, with *backgrnd.gif* in the Image field. Notice the check box underneath the Image field; checking it turns the background image into a *watermark*. While regular background images scroll with the text when the reader uses the scroll bar to move around the page, watermarks are fixed. When the reader scrolls to read text, only the text moves, not the image. This feature is only visible using the Internet Explorer browser; other browsers display a regular background image.

5 Click on the **Do not scroll image** check box to mark it.

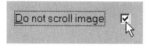

6 Click on the **OK** button.

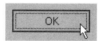

▶ The Background and Links dialog box disappears.

It looks as though nothing is different, but behind the scenes, Internet Assistant has made an important change to the **<BODY>** tag. It has modified the **<BODY>** tag to tell the Web browser to display the file *backgrnd.gif* as the background image instead of the solid color yellow. Let's see how it looks when viewed with Internet Explorer.

7 Select **File** ➤ **Save**.

8 Click on the **Internet Explorer** button in the Taskbar to switch to its viewing window.

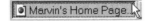

▶ The home page appears, with *backgrnd.gif* tiled to create a uniform background. Scroll around the page to see how the watermark looks. (The background stays fixed while the text appears to move above it.)

Marvin's Magic Shoppe

▶ ▶ ▶ **W**henever you use a background image, choose one that won't compete with or obscure the text on your page.

Changing the Color of Text

Tired of black text with blue hyperlinks? You can use Internet Assistant to set the color of your document's body text, as well as its hyperlinks. This is a great way to give your site a unified, stylish look, especially when the text harmonizes with the background color and pictures in your site.

As with background color, you can choose text color from Internet Assistant's drop-down list of color choices, or you can select other colors by inserting their hexadecimal codes into the HTML source of your document (see the Online Resource for details).

▶ ▶ ▶ The Background and Links command makes color changes to your entire document, whereas the Font command (which you used in Lesson 4) applies color changes only to text you select. If you use the Font command to define sections of text as a particular color, those sections will remain that color even if you use the Background and Links command to give body text and hyperlinks a different color.

Let me caution you: the wrong color choices will turn your site into a visual nightmare for your readers! When using color (for text or the background of your Web pages, or both), I recommend the following guidelines:

- Make sure that the text and background colors look good when used together, and that the text is easy to read.
- Remember that many of your readers have limited color capability, either because their browsers don't recognize color changes, or because their monitors display a limited color range or black and white.
- If your pages have lots of text you want people to read, tend toward more muted color choices.

▶ ▶ ▶ While the above guidelines are written with practicality and convention in mind, I understand that some of you may regard your Web page as your special place for personal expression. If so, use any wacky colors you like, and have fun!

Let's change the color of the text on Marvin's home page.

| 1 | Click on the **Microsoft Word** button in the Taskbar to return to its viewing window. | 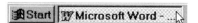 |

2 Select **Format** ➢ **Background and Links.**

▶ The Background and Links dialog box appears. The bottom half of the dialog box is where you can specify changes in text color. As you can see, there are three types of text in a Web page: the body text itself, the hyperlinks that have not yet been viewed, and those that have already been viewed. You can choose to change the color for all three types of text. Let's leave the body text black (so that it's easily readable on our background), and change the color of the hyperlinks.

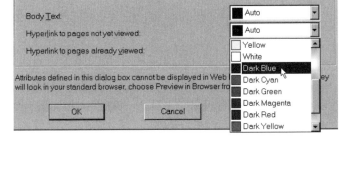

3 Click on the **Hyperlink to pages not yet viewed** field to display a drop-down list of color choices.

4 Select **Dark Blue.**

5 Click on the **Hyperlink to pages already viewed** field and select **Dark Gray.**

6 Click on the **OK** button.

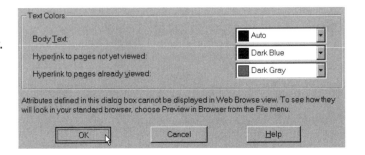

▶ The Background and Links dialog box disappears. Again, nothing looks different in Internet Assistant. Let's view the page in Internet Explorer.

7 Select **File ➣ Save**.

8 Click on the **Internet Explorer** button in the Taskbar to switch to its viewing window.

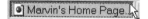

▶ The home page appears, and the color changes show up. In this illustration, I've made one of the hyperlinks on the page already viewed so you can see the color change: the About Marvin's and Tell Marvin What You Think hyperlinks, which haven't yet been viewed, are dark blue, and the Catalog of Wares hyperlink, which has been viewed, is dark gray. Also, notice that "Welcome to Marvin's" is still red (we changed the color of this text using the Font command in Lesson 4).

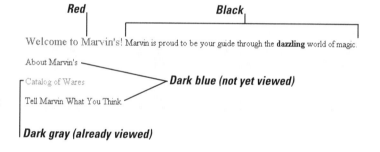

▶ ▶ ▶ **W**hen you make changes to the background and/or text color, they only apply to the Web page you are working on, not to the entire website. For example, if you want *all* of the pages of your website to appear with a yellow background, you need to open each individual HTML document and specify the background color for each one (I'll show you how in the next lesson). This isn't mandatory, of course; you could give your home page a fancy background and leave the rest of the pages plain. Or, if you really wanted to, you could give each page in your site a totally different color scheme.

Adding a Marquee

If you have special announcements or other information you'd like to highlight in your website, a *marquee* is the perfect way to do it. A marquee is a rectangular banner that contains scrolling text. Internet Assistant allows you to control the size and color of the banner, as well as the behavior of the text inside.

 ▶ ▶ ▶ **M**arquees are an extension to HTML specific to the Internet Explorer browser. When viewed in other browsers, marquees appear as regular lines of text.

Let's add a marquee to the home page.

| 1 | Click on the **Microsoft Word** button in the Taskbar to return to its viewing window. |  |

 We'll create a marquee that contains Marvin's special announcements. Let's distinguish it from the list of hyperlinks with a horizontal rule.

2 Place the cursor after **Tell Marvin What You Think.**

About Marvin's

Catalog of Wares

Tell Marvin What You Think

3 Press the ↵ key.

|

4 In the Formatting toolbar, click on the **Horizontal Rule** button.

 A horizontal rule appears on top of the one that you inserted in Lesson 4.

Announcements:

5 Type **Announcements:** and press the ↵ key.

6 Select **Insert ➢ Marquee.**

▶ The Marquee dialog box appears. Here, you specify all of the details necessary to create a marquee. First, let's specify what we would like the marquee to say.

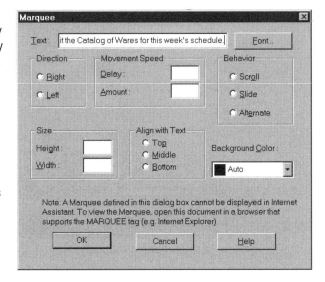

7 In the Text field, type **Attend one of Marvin's free magic workshops! Visit the Catalog of Wares for this week's schedule.**

8 To give the marquee text special formatting attributes, click on the **Font** button.

▶ The Font dialog box appears. This is the same dialog box you used to format text in Lesson 4. As you can see, you can change the font face, color, and size, as well as define it as superscript or sub-script. Let's just change the text color so it really stands out.

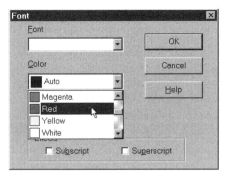

9 Click on the Color field to display a drop-down list of color choices.

10 Select **Red.**

11 Click on the **OK** button.

▶ The Font dialog box
disappears.

The Direction section of the Marquee dialog box controls the direction the text scrolls. The *Right* option creates text that begins at the left side of the marquee and scrolls right, while the *Left* option does the opposite. Left is the better choice in this case, since it will allow visitors to read the announcement from beginning to end as it scrolls by (if we chose Right, the scroll would begin at the left side of the marquee, making our visitors read announcements starting at the end of the sentence).

12 Select the **Left** option
button.

The Movement Speed section controls how fast the text scrolls across the marquee. The *Delay* field controls the speed of the scroll. You enter the number of milliseconds to pause between each successive movement of the marquee text. The smaller the number, the faster the marquee text scrolls by. The *Amount* field controls the smoothness of the scrolling movement. You enter the number of pixels you want the marquee text to move each time. The smaller the number, the slower and smoother the marquee text scrolls.

13 In the Delay field, enter **5.**

14 In the Amount field,
enter **5.**

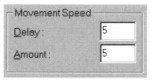

The Behavior section controls how the marquee text scrolls. The *Scroll* option creates continually scrolling text. The *Slide* option creates text that scrolls from one side of the marquee to the other, then stops at the opposite margin and doesn't move again. The *Alternate* option creates text that scrolls from one side of the marquee, and when it reaches the opposite margin, bounces back the other direction.

15 Select the **Scroll** option button.

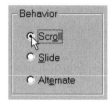

The Size section controls the dimensions of the marquee (in pixels).

16 In the Height field, type **20**.

17 In the Width field, type **250**.

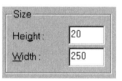

The Align with Text section controls the placement of text within the marquee. You can choose to place text at the top, middle, or bottom of the marquee.

18 Select the **Middle** option.

The Background Color section controls the color of the marquee itself. It will stand in contrast to the background color of the document (unless the colors are the same). If you choose the Auto option (which stands for Automatic), the background color will be whatever your reader's browser's default color is.

19 Click on the Background Color field to display a drop-down list of color choices.

20 Select **Yellow.**

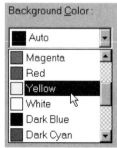

21 Click on the **OK** button.

▶ The Marquee dialog box disappears, and the marquee text appears in your document, blue and underlined. (If you have a relatively small monitor, you may see the warning "DisplayText cannot span more than one line!" If you do, don't worry—it doesn't affect the marquee itself, and you can continue with this example. See the note at the end of this section for an explanation.)

Announcements:

Attend one of Marvin's free magic workshops! Visit the Catalog of Wares...

Since Internet Assistant doesn't know how to display marquees, let's view it in Internet Explorer (remember, other browsers can't display marquees).

22 Select **File** ➣ **Save.**

23 Click on the **Internet Explorer** button in the Taskbar to switch to its viewing window.

▶ The marquee appears. It's a yellow rectangle with Marvin's announcement scrolling toward the left.

Announcements:

Attend one of Marvin's

◀——— *The text is scrolling this direction.*

▶ ▶ ▶ The warning "DisplayText cannot span more than one line!" appears when you create an effect in your Web page that Internet Assistant can't display. These instances include inserting relatively large graphics, inserting graphics or large amounts of text into table cells, and creating marquees with lots of text. The warning may also appear if you magnify your page with the Zoom control (the field on the Standard toolbar that contains a percentage number), or if you have a small monitor. This warning does not affect your page in any way and will disappear when you view your page in another Web browser. For more explanation, consult the Internet Assistant Help system.

Adding Background Sound

One of Internet Explorer's more whimsical features is the ability to play a *background sound* when someone visits one of your Web pages. As soon as a reader visits the page, the sound of your choice can greet them—perhaps a lively musical interlude or the voice of your CEO welcoming them to the site.

Internet Explorer is able to play any sound that is saved in the WAV, AU, or MIDI sound file formats (they have the file name extensions *.wav, .au,* and *.mid*). As when you insert a picture, Internet Assistant allows you to create a relative link between your HTML document and the sound file to create a background sound.

▶ ▶ ▶ Adding sounds to your Web page (and inline video clips, which I'll talk about later in this lesson) significantly increases its load time. For this reason, make sure that files you include are as small as possible.

There are lots of sounds available all over the Web—from your favorite Bart Simpson quote to clips from the original *War of the Worlds* radio program (visit the Online Resource for links to a bunch of shareware sound archives). You can also record your own sound using Sound Recorder, an accessory that is included with Windows 95.

To properly record and hear sounds, you must have sound equipment installed on your computer: a sound card, speakers, and a microphone or other audio input device (such as a CD-ROM drive).

 ▶ ▶ ▶ **B**ackground sound is an extension to HTML specific to the Internet Explorer browser. Your readers must be using Internet Explorer and have sound equipment installed on their computers to be able to hear background sounds in your Web pages.

Let's add a background sound to Marvin's home page: a personal welcome from Marvin himself.

1 Click on the **Microsoft Word** button in the Taskbar to return to its viewing window.

2 Click on the **<BODY...>** tag.

3 Press the ← key to place the cursor before the **<BODY...>** tag (the note at the end of this section explains why you're placing the cursor here).

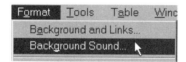

4 Select **Format ➣ Background Sound.**

▶ The Background Sound dialog box appears. The first thing to do is to specify the sound file itself.

5 Click on the **Browse** button.

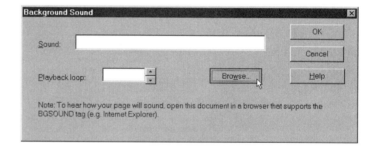

▶ The Sound File to Use dialog box appears and displays all of the sound files available in your My Documents folder.

6 Double-click on **welcome.wav.**

▶ The Sound File to Use dialog box disappears, and the Background Sound dialog box becomes visible again, with *welcome.wav* in the Sound field.

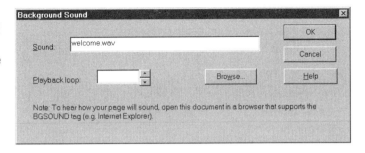

▶ The Playback loop field allows you to specify how many times you'd like the sound to repeat when someone visits the page. You can select a number by clicking on the up-arrow of the field, or by entering a number up to 999. If you'd like the sound to play continuously until the reader leaves the page, you can click on the field's down-arrow to select INFINITE.

7 Click once on the up-arrow to select **1**.

8 Click on the **OK** button.

▶ The Background Sound dialog box disappears, and the **<BGSOUND>** tag appears in your document to remind you that you have added a background sound.

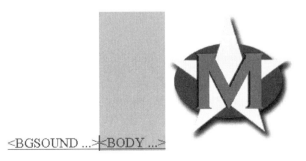

Let's switch to Internet Explorer to hear the sound (you need to have sound equipment installed in your computer in order to do so).

9 Select **File** ➤ **Save**.

10 Click on the **Internet Explorer** button in the Taskbar to switch to its viewing window.

▶ "Welcome to Marvin's Magic Shoppe!" plays as soon as the document window appears.

"Welcome to — Marvin's Magic Shoppe!"

Marvin's Magic Shoppe

▶ ▶ ▶ In this example, I had you insert the `<BGSOUND>` tag before the `<BODY...>` tag. While the Background Sound feature will work no matter where the tag appears in the document, the tag itself tends to get lost in the clutter of the page. This way, the tag is clearly visible at the top of the page and is easy to find if you'd like to alter it. (To alter it, double-click on the tag, and the Background Sound dialog box will appear again, letting you make any changes you like.)

Adding a Video Clip

In Lesson 6, we added inline images to your website. Internet Assistant lets you go a step further by adding inline *video clips* to your HTML documents as well. Video clips are essentially images that move; they can be a small section of movie footage, say, or an animated graphic. When viewed with Internet Explorer, a video clip, like an inline image, sits within the Web page, and plays either when the page is opened or when the reader passes the cursor over it.

 ▶ ▶ ▶ **I**nline video clips are an extension to HTML and are only visible in Internet Explorer. Other browsers display an "unknown graphic" symbol in place of the inline video clip.

Inline video clips must be saved in the AVI file format to be visible in Internet Explorer (the file name extension is *.avi*). Unfortunately, at the time of this writing there aren't any public-domain video galleries, as there are for GIF and JPG images. If you want to include video clips in your Web pages, you'll need access to commercial or shareware animation software to convert graphics into moving pictures and to save them as AVIs (as always, the Online Resource is a good place to start). If you want to put video footage from your Himalayan trekking adventure onto your home page, you'll need additional hardware called a *video capture card* and its accompanying software to be able to convert video into digital information.

I've included a sample AVI on the CD: *marvin.avi*. This is a miniature, animated version of Marvin's company logo. Let's add it to Marvin's home page.

1	Click on the **Microsoft Word** button in the Taskbar to return to the Internet Assistant viewing window.

2 Scroll to the bottom of the home page's viewing window.

3 Place the cursor directly in front of the first line of Marvin's address.

Marvin's Magic Shoppe
1000 Main Street
Funplace, USA 10101

4 Press the ↵ key to create a new line, then place the cursor in the space just created.

| I

Marvin's Magic Shoppe
1000 Main Street
Funplace, USA 10101

5 In the Formatting toolbar, click on the **Picture** button.

▶ The Picture dialog box appears. This is the same dialog box you used in Lesson 6 to create inline images.

6 Click on the **Video** tab at the top of the dialog box to make those options visible.

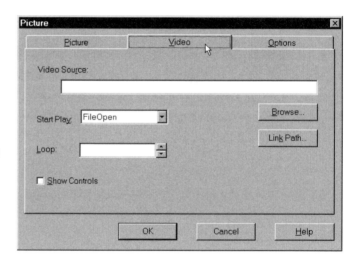

▶ This section contains everything you need to insert an inline video clip. The Video Source field allows you to create a relative link to an AVI file on your server or an absolute link to one stored in a remote location on the Web.

7 Click on the **Browse** button.

▶ The Video File to Link dialog box appears and displays all of the AVI files in your My Documents folder.

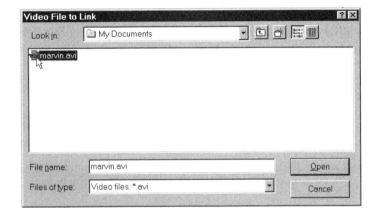

8 Double-click on **marvin.avi.**

▶ The Video File to Link dialog box disappears, and the Picture dialog box becomes visible again, with *marvin.avi* in the Video Source field.

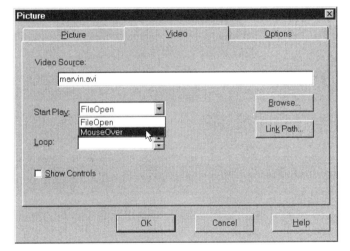

▶ The Start Play field allows you to specify when the video begins playing. To have the video play immediately when the reader opens the page, select the FileOpen option. To have the video play when the reader moves the cursor over the image, select the MouseOver option.

9 Click on the Start Play field to display a drop-down list of options.

10   Select **MouseOver**.

▶   The Loop field allows you to control the number of times you'd like the video to automatically repeat itself. You can enter a number up to 999, or you can have the video play continuously by clicking on the field's down-arrow to select INFINITE.

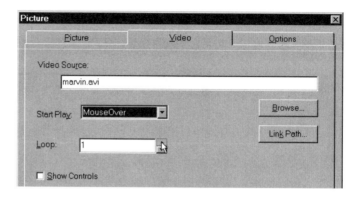

11   Click once on the up-arrow to select **1**.

▶   The Show Controls check-box allows you to display control buttons in the Web page that allow the readers to stop and start the video play themselves. The controls appear beneath the inline video clip. We'll leave this option unmarked.

You have all of Internet Assistant's picture tools at your disposal when creating inline video clips, including the Size and Border controls in the Options section of the dialog box, and the Alternate text control in the Picture section of the dialog box. Let's add alternate text to the video clip, so that those of your readers not using Internet Explorer will at least know what they are missing.

12 Click on the **Picture** tab at the top of the dialog box.

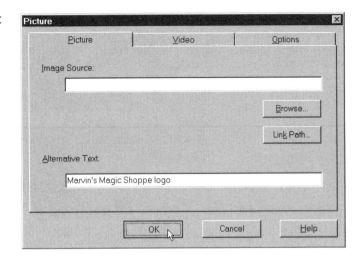

▶ The Picture section of the dialog box becomes visible.

13 In the Alternative Text field, type **Marvin's Magic Shoppe logo.**

14 Click on the **OK** button.

▶ The Picture dialog box disappears, and alternative text appears in your document at the location of the inline video clip.

Marvin's Magic Shoppe logo

Marvin's Magic Shoppe
1000 Main Street
Funplace, USA 10101

Since Internet Assistant can't display video, let's see how it looks in Internet Explorer.

15 Select **File ➢ Save.**

16 Click on the **Internet Explorer** button in the Taskbar to switch to its viewing window.

The video appears in the home page. When you pass the cursor over the image, it rotates once.

The logo spins around.

Marvin's Magic Shoppe
1000 Main Street
Funplace, USA 10101

Inserting HTML Tags Manually

HTML is an ever-changing language, with new tags and extensions being added all the time. The creators of Internet Assistant (being the smart people they are) understand this and have built a catch-all into the program that lets you insert HTML tags yourself. That way, when a new tag comes along (or if you want to use one that exists now but that Internet Assistant doesn't support), you can use it in your document easily enough.

Of course, to insert tags, you need to know what they *are,* which means that you need to learn a bit of HTML. If this prospect scares you, remember, it's *optional.* Internet Assistant includes built-in support for every HTML tag you need to build a great Web page. But, if you want to push the envelope of Web design, Internet Assistant won't hold you back.

  The Online Resource includes links to the latest HTML tags and extensions so you can always keep up-to-date.

There are two ways to manually insert HTML tags into your document: by using the Insert HTML Markup command and by inserting text directly into the HTML source of your document. The following examples will show you how to do both.

Creating Custom Horizontal Rules

Remember horizontal rules? They're the lines you can use as dividers or design elements in your pages. Browser-specific extensions exist that allow you to vary the look of the horizontal rule. You can use these extensions to change its width, thickness, and alignment on the page. When you use Internet Assistant's Insert Horizontal Rule command, however, you have only one choice: you get a rule that extends the width of the page.

▶ ▶ ▶ **B**rowsers that don't recognize these extensions display custom horizontal rules like all of the others: they span the width of the page and are of uniform size and thickness.

We'll use Internet Assistant's Insert HTML Markup command to replace a regular horizontal rule with one that is customized.

1	Click on the **Microsoft Word** button in the Taskbar to return to the Internet Assistant viewing window.	

2	With your cursor, select the horizontal rule above Marvin's address.	*Marvin's Magic Shoppe* *1000 Main Street* *Funplace, USA 10101*

3	Press the **Delete** key.	*Marvin's Magic Shoppe* *1000 Main Street* *Funplace, USA 10101*
▶	The horizontal rule disappears.	

4 Select **Insert ➤ HTML Markup.**

▶ The Insert HTML Markup dialog box appears. Here, you enter the tag you would like to insert, including the brackets that surround the tag. We'll enter the tag for a horizontal rule that is left-aligned and 250 pixels wide.

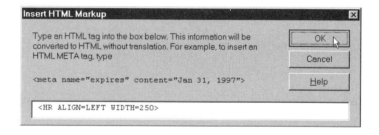

5 Enter **<HR ALIGN= LEFT WIDTH=250>.**

6 Click on the **OK** button.

▶ The Insert HTML Markup dialog box disappears, and the tag itself appears as blue, underlined text to remind you that you inserted a tag Internet Assistant can't display.

<u>*<HR ALIGN=LEFT WIDTH=250>*</u>*Marvin's Magic Shoppe
1000 Main Street
Funplace, USA 10101*

7 Press the ↵ key to place the tag on its own line.

<HR ALIGN=LEFT WIDTH=250>

Marvin's Magic Shoppe
1000 Main Street
Funplace, USA 10101

Let's see how it looks in Internet Explorer.

8 Select **File** ➤ **Save.**

9 Click on the **Internet Explorer** button in the Taskbar to switch to its viewing window.

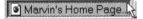

▶ The document appears, complete with a custom horizontal rule.

Marvin's Magic Shoppe
1000 Main Street
Funplace, USA 10101

▶ ▶ ▶ **W**hen inserting HTML markup, you can use upper- or lowercase letters in the HTML tag. I use uppercase letters, since that's what Internet Assistant does, and it makes the HTML source easier to read as a result.

▶ ▶ ▶ **W**hile using upper- or lowercase characters is fine for HTML tags, when creating links (hyperlinks, or links between graphic, video, or sound files), you *must* use the identical case used in the file name. For example, if you created a hyperlink in your document to *MARVIN.HTM*, but the file's name is *marvin.htm*, the hyperlink would not work. For that reason, I always name my files with lowercase letters, so I don't have to think about the case of the file name when I use it in a link.

Adding Alternative Fonts

In Lesson 4, I talked about how you can use the Font command to liven up your Web pages with a custom font. The font (or fonts) you choose, however, must be present on your readers' computers for them to be visible on their screens. If they aren't present, the text will be displayed in their browser's default font (usually Times New Roman).

You can list several fonts as alternatives in case your first choice is not available on your reader's computer. Let's do that now, but instead of using the Insert HTML Markup command, we'll make the change directly to the HTML source.

1 Click on the **Microsoft Word** button in the Taskbar to return to the Internet Assistant viewing window.

2 Highlight the page banner that reads **Marvin's Magic Shoppe.**

3 Select **Format ➤ Font.**

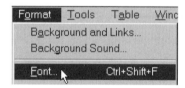

▶ The Font dialog box appears.

4 Click on the Font field and select **Arial.**

5 Click on the **OK** button.

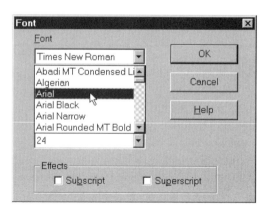

▶ The Font dialog box disappears, and the page banner's font changes from Times New Roman to Arial.

In case some of your readers don't have Arial in their font directory, let's add an alternative to the list of fonts that can be displayed in its place.

6 Select **View** ➤ **HTML Source.**

▶ The View HTML Tags dialog box appears saying that you must save the changes to your document in order to view HTML source.

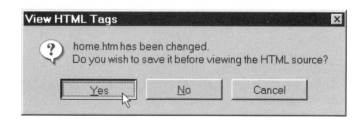

7 Click on the **Yes** button.

▶ There is a pause as Word saves the changes to your document and switches views, then the HTML source of your document becomes visible.

|<HTML>

<HEAD>

<TITLE>Marvin's Home Page</TITLE>

8 Scroll down until you see the home page banner.

▶ The font size and face are indicated in the HTML source with the opening tag **<FONT SIZE=6 FACE="Arial">**, and the closing tag **</FONT>**. We'll now add the font Helvetica to the list that will display in the event that Arial is not present on the reader's computer.

`<H1><CENTER><FONT SIZE=6 FACE="Arial">Marvin's Magic Shoppe`
`</FONT></CENTER></H1>`

9 Place the cursor directly after the word **Arial** and before the closing quotation mark.

`<H1><CENTER><FONT SIZE=6 FACE="Arial">Marvin's Magic Shoppe`
`</FONT></CENTER></H1>`

10 Type **,Helvetica.**

`<H1><CENTER><FONT SIZE=6 FACE="Arial,Helvetica">Marvin's Magic Shoppe`
`</FONT></CENTER></H1>`

11 Click on the **Return to Edit Mode** button to return to HTML Edit view.

▶ The Close HTML dialog box appears, asking if you would like to save the changes you've made to the document's HTML source.

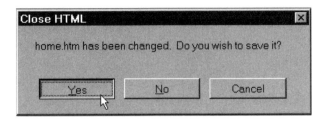

12 Click on the **Yes** button.

There is a pause
as Internet Assistant
switches back to HTML
Edit view, and in a
moment your document
reappears.

Some of the document's elements may look different now. That's
because viewing HTML source and returning to HTML Edit view has
the same effect as closing and opening the document. For more details,
refer to the section of the Internet Assistant Help system titled "Frequently
Asked Questions" and read the answer to the question "Why does my
Internet Assistant document look different after I close and reopen it?"
Remember, you can always preview your document in another browser
to see what it will look like to the majority of your readers once it is published on the Web.

I've only described a couple of the creative things you can do with a little knowledge
of HTML. There are plenty more for you to explore and experiment with as your Web
publishing expertise grows.

Don't forget to view HTML source every time your websurfing takes you
to a well-designed site. The tricks you pick up from the experts can later
be used in your own documents!

For now, though, it's break time.

1 Select **File** ➢ **Exit** and save the document as an HTML file. (If you feel like moving on to the next lesson right now, select File ➢ Save All.)

▶ Word saves your document and shuts down, and your desktop reappears.

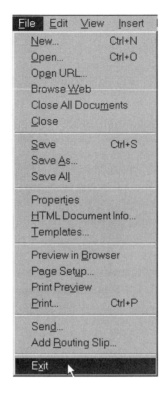

In this lesson, you've picked up a few expert tricks to make your Web pages look great. In the next lesson, you'll give your website the final touches to prepare for its worldwide debut.

PART FOUR

GOING PUBLIC

PUTTING THE FINISHING TOUCHES ON YOUR WEBSITE

You've put a lot of hard work and creativity into your home page, and you're ready (and excited, no doubt) to share it with the rest of the world. Before you make your pages "live," however, there are a few last-minute checks you must do. You want your home page to reflect your (and/or your company's) skill, professionalism, and attention to detail. Incorrect hyperlinks, graphics that don't load, and everyday details such as spelling and grammar errors tell your readers that you haven't taken the time to make sure your website is perfect.

In this lesson, we'll give Marvin's home page the white glove treatment. We'll test all of the hyperlinks, finish the menu bar and copy it onto each page, standardize the layout and design, and clean up all of the final details. When we're done, Marvin's website will be ready for public viewing.

Standardizing the Design

The first thing to do is to make sure that all of your pages have a consistent look. This includes standardizing the color scheme for each page and making sure that the page banners look the same (or at least complement each other).

Standardizing the Color Scheme

First, let's make the color scheme the same for all of the pages in Marvin's site.

1 Open Word by clicking on the **Start** button and selecting **Microsoft Word.**

Word Popens and presents you with a blank document.

2 Select **File** ➢ **Open**.

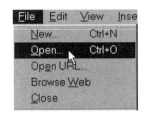

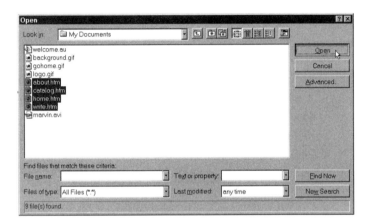

The Open dialog box appears and displays the contents of your My Documents folder. Since we'll be working with all of your Web pages in this lesson, let's open all of them at once.

3 While holding down the Shift key, click on **about.htm**, **catalog.htm**, **home.htm**, and **write.htm** to select them.

4 Click on the **Open** button.

All of the pages open. Let's start with the home page.

5 Select **Window** ➢ **home.htm**.

▶ Marvin's home page appears. With Word's Copy and Paste commands, you can copy the logo to each page and standardize the color scheme in one step. All you need to do is to copy the logo graphic *and* the **<BODY...>** tag, and paste it at the top of each page.

6 Using your cursor, highlight **<BODY...>** and the logo graphic.

7 Select **Edit** ➢ **Copy** (alternatively, click on the **Copy** tool in the Standard toolbar or use the keyboard shortcut **Ctrl+C**).

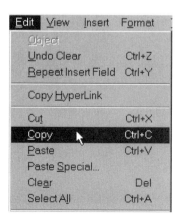

8   Select **Window ➢ about.htm** to move to that document.

9   Select **Edit ➢ Paste** (or click on the **Paste** tool in the Standard toolbar or use the keyboard shortcut **Ctrl+V**).

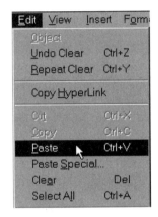

▶   The **<BODY...>** tag and the logo appear at the top of *about.htm*.

<BODY ...>

About Marvin's

10 Now do the same with *catalog.htm* and *write.htm* (I won't illustrate it here since the procedure is exactly the same)…and your pages' color schemes will be standardized!

What could be easier?

▶ ▶ ▶ **Y**ou can also take advantage of Word's drag-and-drop editing feature to copy and paste information. To do so, arrange the viewing windows of the source and destination documents on your screen so they are all visible. Select the text and/or graphics you want to copy. Hold down the Ctrl key, click on the selected area, and hold down the mouse button. Your cursor will turn into a pointer with a little + sign next to it. Drag the pointer to the new location in the other document (still holding down the Ctrl key), and release the mouse button and the Ctrl key. The selected text and/or graphics will appear in the new document.

Standardizing the Banner Font

In Lesson 9, we gave the home page banner a custom font. Let's apply that font (Arial) to the banners of the other Web pages.

1 If you're not already there, select **Window ➤ about.htm.**

2 Select the page banner at the top of *about.htm*.

3 Select **Format** ➤ **Font.**

4 Click on the Font field to display a drop-down list of choices.

5 Select **Arial.**

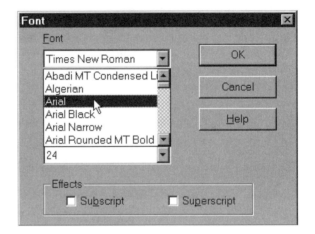

6 Click on the **OK** button.

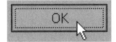

▶ The "About Marvin's" page banner is displayed in Arial font.

7 Now do the same with *catalog.htm* and *write.htm* so that all of the page banners look consistent.

Transferring the Menu Bar to All of Your Pages

In Lesson 5, we created a menu bar containing hyperlinks to every page in the website. This menu bar sits at the bottom of each page as a navigational aid for your readers. Now, let's copy it from *about.htm* and paste it into the rest of your pages.

1 If you're not already there, select **Window** ➢ **about.htm.**

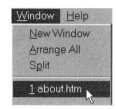

2 Scroll down to the bottom of the page to make the menu bar visible.

 About Marvin's | Catalog of Wares | Write to Marvin

3 Highlight the entire menu bar, including the graphic hyperlink.

4 Select **Edit** ➢ **Copy.**

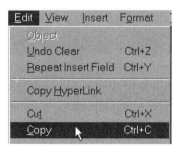

5 Select **Window ➤ catalog.htm.**

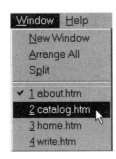

6 Scroll down until the bottom of the page is visible.

- The Auto-Reshuffler: you'll never have to shuffle again
- The Disappearing Jack: amaze your friends with this classic trick

7 In order to paste the menu bar at the bottom of the document, you need to insert some space underneath the last line on the page. Place the cursor directly after the word **trick** and press ⏎.

▶ A new, blank item in the bulleted list appears.

- The Auto-Reshuffler: you'll never have to shuffle again
- The Disappearing Jack: amaze your friends with this classic trick
- |

8 Let's remove the bullet by defining that line as normal text. From the Style box, select **Normal, P.**

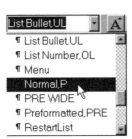

▶ The bullet disappears.

9 Select **Edit** ➢ **Paste.**

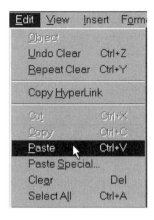

▶ The menu bar appears at the bottom of *catalog.htm.*

• The Auto-Reshuffler: you'll never have to shuffle again

• The Disappearing Jack: amaze your friends with this classic trick

 About Marvin's | Catalog of Wares | Write to Marvin

10 Select **Window** ➢ **write.htm.**

11 Scroll to the bottom of the page and place the cursor directly after the word *Form* in the "Bottom of Form" boundary message.

Bottom of Form

12 Press ↵ to add space after the form boundary.

13 Select **Edit** ➤ **Paste**.

▶ The menu bar appears at the bottom of the form.

Bottom of Form

 About Marvin's | Catalog of Wares | Write to Marvin

 ▶ ▶ ▶ **W**henever you add text to a Web page that contains a form, unless it is part of the form itself, add the text outside of the form boundaries.

Now your readers will be able to navigate throughout Marvin's website from each page.

Double-Checking Your Hyperlinks

The binding threads of your website are the hyperlinks you've included in each of your Web pages. Before you make your page public, check *each and every* hyperlink to make sure that it's active and that it works properly. You should read through each page carefully to check for links you may have forgotten along the way. If you can recruit a willing friend to be your second pair of eyes, so much the better.

Let's test the links in Marvin's site to make sure they work.

▶ ▶ ▶ **Y**ou need to establish your internet connection right now in order to test the hyperlink to Magic Central on the About Marvin's page.

1 Select **Window** ➢ **home.htm**.

2 Double-click on **About Marvin's**.

●

● Catalog of Wares

● Tell Marvin What You Think

▶ *about.htm* appears, letting you know that your link works.

3 Double-click on **magic**.

's Magic Shoppe is th
dreamed of ▮▮▮. H
ged his natural curios

▶ You jump to the location of the magic bookmark.

 Any mysterious, seemingly inexplicable, or extraordinary power or quality

illusion: Something that appears to be what it's not

You get the idea. Test every single link in your entire website to make sure it does what it's supposed to do. If you run into any surprises, examine the problem by highlighting the ailing link and clicking on the Hyperlink button. You can then double-check the link details and correct them if necessary.

▶ ▶ ▶ **T**o make quick corrections to the hyperlink references in your document, use the HTML Hidden button (the one with an *a* inside red brackets on it) in the Standard toolbar. Clicking on this button instantly displays certain HTML attributes, like hyperlink references, allowing you to edit them without having to view HTML source.

Making Sure All of Your Documents Are Titled

Titles are easy to overlook, since your pages will work perfectly well without them. Nevertheless, titles on every page of your site are an important part of your website's overall image.

1 If you're not already there, select **Window ➢ home.htm** to move to the home page.

2 In the Formatting toolbar, click on the **Title** tool.

▶ The HTML Document Head Information dialog box appears. As you can see, this document has a perfectly good title.

3 Click on the **OK** button.

Now, check the titles on the rest of your pages. If you run into any titles you don't like, you can change them now. If you run into any untitled documents, you can enter an appropriate title.

  Another wonderful advantage of using Internet Assistant is that you have access to all of Word's timesaving correction tools for use in your HTML documents. Take advantage of Word's spell and grammar checking features before you make your pages public. Why let a typo or incorrect usage mar your work of art?

You're now ready to go! Time to exit Word and either take a break or jump right into the next lesson.

1 Select **File** ➤ **Exit** and respond to the dialog boxes that appear, saving each of your files as HTML documents. (If you'd like to move on, select File ➤ Save All.)

► Word saves your documents, shuts down, and your desktop reappears.

You've now given your website a thorough once-over, and you're ready for "prime time!" In the next lesson, we'll talk about how to transfer your pages to your Internet service provider's Web server. Once your home page is "live," I'll give you some tips on how to let the rest of the world know about it and how to keep it up-to-date.

11

PUTTING YOUR PAGES ON THE WEB

Here **it is**…the moment you've been waiting for. Time to "go live" and make your home page accessible on the Web. In this lesson, I'll talk about how to transfer your home page files to your Internet service provider's Web server. Once there, I'll give you some easy tips on how to let the rest of the world know you're ready for visitors. Finally, I'll show you how to make changes to your site once it's public.

Uploading Your Home Page Files

Transferring, or *uploading*, your home page files to your Internet service provider's Web server is a simple matter of using an FTP program. As I mentioned in Lesson 1, FTP software lets you transfer files to and from computers over the Internet. Most providers give you an FTP program as part of your Internet service.

  If you don't have an FTP program, or if you're not sure how to use the one you do have, contact your provider's customer service staff for their recommendations. I include links in the Online Resource to several popular FTP programs that are available on the Internet.

I use an FTP program called IFTP32. If you use a different program, don't worry; your screen will look different, but the basic functions are the same.

Before you begin, you need to get a few details from your Internet service provider. These details are probably posted on their home page; if not, give them a call. You need to know:

- Where to store your home page files on their Web server
- What file name to give the initial (home) page of your site
- The URL of your home page once it's public

Where to Store Your Home Page Files

Your Internet service provider has set aside a special directory on the Web server to store your home page files and make them accessible to everyone on the Web. You need to find out *where* that directory is. For example, my Internet service provider supplies all of its users with a personal directory on its Web server called a *public HTML* directory in which to store home page files. Everything I store in my public HTML directory is visible to anyone who wants to see it.

Home Page File Name

Most Internet service providers require that you give the initial page of your website a specific name (examples include *home.htm, index.htm,* and *default.htm*). That name tells the Web server that it's the default page for that directory and that it should load automatically if someone requests that directory while browsing.

For example, the URL of my personal home page is **http://www.dnai.com/~asha**. The "~asha" part of the URL tells the reader's Web browser to request my home page from my public HTML directory on the Web server. When the server receives the request, it checks my directory for the presence of a document called *index.htm*, and loads it automatically. If I *didn't* have a document called *index.htm* stored there, the reader wouldn't see a Web page, but rather a display of all of the files stored in my public HTML directory (not very attractive).

▶ ▶ ▶ If your Internet service provider requires you to name your home page something other than *home.htm* (say, *index.htm* for example), you need to do two things: first, select File ➤ Save As and replace the file name *home* with *index*, and, second, update the hyperlinks in your HTML documents that point to *home.htm* to point instead to *index.htm*.

Your Home Page URL

Finally, find out what the URL of your home page will be once it's live. That way, you can start publicizing your site as soon as it's public.

Once you have these details in hand, you're ready to begin.

 ▶ ▶ ▶ **T**o continue with this lesson, you need to activate your Internet connection.

1 Open your FTP program by clicking on the **Start** button and selecting its icon.

▶ Your FTP program opens and presents you with a connection dialog box.

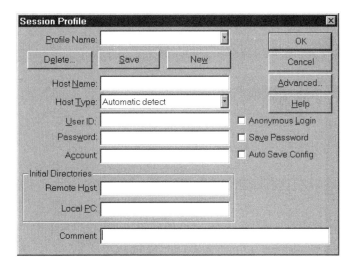

Okay, let's stop here and take a look at what's on the screen. All FTP programs require basic information to be able to transfer files to and from computers on the Internet.

- *Host Name:* The host name is the name of the server to which you are transferring your home page files.
- *User ID:* When you signed on for Internet service, your provider had you choose a user ID name (also called a *user name*, or a *login name*) and a password to be able to access your account. You must specify your user ID to be able to access the Web server with your FTP program.
- *Password:* You also need to specify your password to be able to access the server.
- *Remote Host:* Some FTP programs allow you to specify the destination directory to which you'll be uploading files as soon as you log on. Others have you log on to the server first, then navigate to the correct directory on the Web server (very much like using the Windows Explorer to navigate around the directories on your hard drive).
- *Local PC:* Some FTP programs also allow you to specify the directory on your hard drive that contains the files you want to upload.

Now, let's log on to the Web server and upload your home page files.

 ► ► ► The following examples illustrate how I upload home page files to *my* Internet service provider, so the details such as host name, user ID, etc. are different than yours. Simply substitute your own information as you go through the example.

1 In the Host Name field, enter the name of your Internet service provider's Web server.

2 In the User ID field, enter your user ID.

3 In the Password field, enter your password.

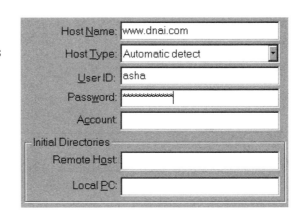

4 If your FTP program has a Remote Host field, enter the path to your destination directory (the directory your Internet service provider has set aside to store your home page files).

5 If your FTP program allows you to specify the location on your hard drive of the files you'll be uploading, enter **\My Documents.**

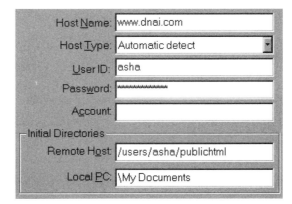

6 Activate your FTP connection.

▶ A window opens, displaying your FTP session.

Now that your FTP session is active, you can transfer your home page files from your computer to your Internet service provider's Web server. With IFTP32, the process is similar to using the Windows Explorer to copy files to different locations on your hard drive. On the left, you see the contents of your My Documents folder, while on the right, you see your (now empty) destination directory on the Web server. All you have to do is transfer the files from one location to the other.

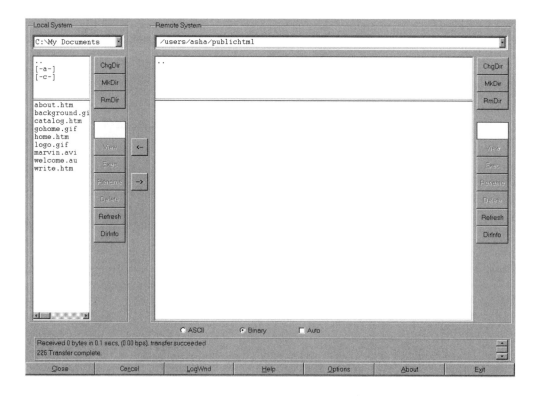

The only detail you need to remember is to specify the type of files you're transferring. HTML files, since they are nothing more than plain text (also referred to as *ASCII text*), should be transferred in ASCII mode. Graphics (and any other type of home page file, such as sounds and videos) are called *binary files*, and should be transferred in binary mode.

▶ ▶ ▶ **D**ifferent FTP programs refer to ASCII and binary modes using other terms. If you're in doubt, read your FTP program's documentation, or call your Internet service provider's customer service staff.

First, let's transfer your HTML files.

1 Select each of your HTML files by clicking on them while holding down the Ctrl key.

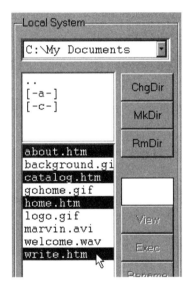

2 Specify that you are transferring ASCII files.

3 Initiate the transfer.

▶ Your HTML files are copied to the Web server. Once the transfer is complete, the names of the files appear in your destination directory.

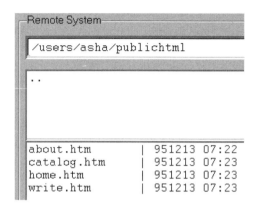

```
Remote System

/users/asha/publichtml

..

about.htm    | 951213 07:22
catalog.htm  | 951213 07:23
home.htm     | 951213 07:23
write.htm    | 951213 07:23
```

Now let's transfer your graphic, sound, and video files.

1 Select all of the other files by clicking on them while holding down the Ctrl key.

```
about.htm
background.gi
catalog.htm
gohome.gif
home.htm
logo.gif
marvin.avi
welcome.wav
write.htm
```

2 Specify that you are transferring binary files.

Binary

3 Initiate the transfer.

▶ Your graphic, sound, and video files are copied to the Web server. Once the transfer is complete, the names of the files appear in your destination directory.

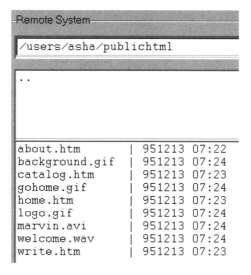

```
Remote System

/users/asha/publichtml


..



about.htm        | 951213 07:22
background.gif    | 951213 07:24
catalog.htm       | 951213 07:23
gohome.gif        | 951213 07:24
home.htm          | 951213 07:23
logo.gif          | 951213 07:24
marvin.avi        | 951213 07:24
welcome.wav       | 951213 07:24
write.htm         | 951213 07:23
```

4 Exit your FTP program.

Congratulations! Your website is now visible to millions of websurfers everywhere, and you can call yourself a real Web publisher!

▶ ▶ ▶ **E**ven though you double-checked your home page before uploading it, it's a good idea to make sure everything is working as it should now that it's live. Take a look at your website at its new URL with a Web browser, and give each page a final survey to be sure it's perfect. If you notice a problem such as a hyperlink that doesn't work or a graphic that doesn't load, correct your original HTML file (the one on your computer), and upload it again. You'll read more about making changes to your website once it's public later in this lesson.

Announcing Yourself to the World

Now that your website is "up," you'll want to be sure to let everyone know about it. The great thing about the Internet is that you don't need to take out an expensive magazine or television ad to publicize your home page (even though plenty of big companies do). There are many easy (and free) ways to spread the word about your website. All you need is a little know-how, some tact, and some time.

  I've devoted a section of the Online Resource to website publicity. There, you'll find links to popular search utilities and other places to list your site.

The first stop on your virtual publicity tour should be one (or all) of the Web's search utilities. Whenever a websurfer wants to find something, he or she goes there first. Most search utilities have an easy form, similar to the one shown here, that you can fill out to add your URL to the list.

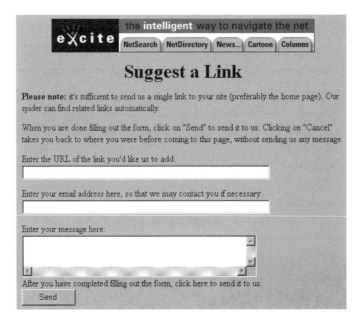

Once you've listed yourself there, start searching for *any* other place on the Web that would consider posting a link back to your site. Send a politely-worded e-mail message to the site's administrator including your site's URL, and explaining why you think their visitors would appreciate a link to your site. Perhaps your Internet service provider has a special listing for its business sites. Maybe you have friends and colleagues who would include a link to your home page from theirs. With a keen eye and a little patience, you can find lots of places on the Web that would be happy to add a link on their home page to yours.

Add the URL of your home page to the *signature line* of your e-mail messages. A signature is a bit of text that is automatically appended to each of your messages by your e-mail program (check your e-mail program's documentation to learn how to create a signature). Each e-mail message you send will be transformed into a tiny traveling advertisement if you include your URL along with a subtle but enticing invitation to visit at the bottom of each one:

```
--------------------------------------------------------------
Visit Marvin's Magic Shoppe at http://www.magic.com/~marvin
--------------------------------------------------------------
```

Another way to spread the word is to post a brief announcement on selected Usenet newsgroups that cater to readers who may find your site interesting or helpful. For example, Marvin may choose to become a regular on the *alt.magic* newsgroup, and post a message announcing his site there. If you decide to do this, be sure to follow the rules of *netiquette:*

- Only post announcements to newsgroups that address topics related to your website. Posting to unrelated newsgroups (called *spamming*) is considered rude, and will invariably result in hostile e-mail and bad publicity.
- Once you find a newsgroup to which you'd like to post your announcement, read it regularly for a week or so to get a feel for it (called *lurking* in Net-speak). This way, you can gauge how receptive the newsgroup's readership will be to your post.
- Indicate that you are announcing your website in the subject line of your e-mail message. For example, the subject line of Marvin's announcement could read: **ANNOUNCE: Marvin's Magic Shoppe is online!**
- When writing your announcement, keep it short and respectful. Steer clear of marketing hype language; instead, issue a polite invitation to newsgroup readers to visit your site and tell them what they will find there.
- Make sure to include your website's URL and your e-mail address.

If you follow these rules to the letter and *still* receive a few insulting e-mail messages (or *flames* as they are better known), don't take it personally. There are still plenty of netizens out there who resent any commercial use of the Internet and won't hesitate to let you know in colorful terms.

Finally, use whatever traditional methods of publicity you have at your disposal. Add your website's URL and your e-mail address to your business cards and letterhead. If you have any type of print advertising, include them there as well.

Keeping Your Pages Up-to-Date

Once your home page is live and you've publicized it, you're sure to get lots of visitors. To keep those visitors coming over the long term, you need to keep the content of your website fresh and up-to-date. This means making regular changes to your website, adding new pages when appropriate, and letting folks know what's new on your website.

  Many websites devote an entire page to listing what's new on the website and announcing current news.

For example, if Marvin gets a lot of response from his website, he may want to expand the Catalog of Wares page to include his entire inventory. Or he may want to create an online ordering system. For fun, he may want to sponsor a contest that encourages his readers to send him feedback, with prizes for the winner.

Updating your website is easy: you simply make any changes you want to the original HTML files on your computer, save them, and upload them to the Web server. The new versions (as long as they have identical names) will automatically replace the old versions of the files that are already stored there.

Adding new pages to your site is just as simple. Create a new HTML document with Internet Assistant, make sure its design is consistent with the other pages, and integrate it into the rest of your website by adding links to it from the home page and from the text menu bar. Once you're done, upload *all* of the pages you've changed to the Web server again.

 ▶ ▶ ▶ **E**ach time you make changes to your home page, be sure to test it to make sure all of the hyperlinks and graphics work properly.

Congratulations! You've reached the end of this book, and you have a beautiful home page to show for it. You've experienced how easy Internet Assistant makes Web publishing, and you now have all the skills and tools you need to create your own personal or business home page. You can use Marvin's Magic Shoppe as a model upon which to publish your own company's website. Perhaps you'd like to create a professional-looking online résumé to impress potential employers. Or maybe you just want to tell the world about your famous lasagna recipe or your seven cats. The possibilities are endless. The Online Resource contains links all over the Web that will help you expand your Web publishing knowledge, and provide you with inspiration and ideas for new projects. Fire up Internet Assistant, and remember, the World (Wide Web) is your oyster!

APPENDICES

APPENDIX A

GETTING AN
INTERNET CONNECTION

If you want to publish on the World Wide Web, the first step is to get an Internet connection. Happily, it's easier now than ever. Setting up Internet service to your home or office can be about as simple as getting a second phone line.

In this appendix, I'll detail the types of service and software you need in order to publish documents on the Web. I'll also talk about how to go about choosing an Internet service provider. Finally, I'll give you a list of questions to ask while you're comparison shopping to make sure you get the best value for your money.

  I'm assuming you already have the hardware you need; that is, a computer and a modem (or other connection device). If not, read the review sections of the popular computer magazines and ask your friends and colleagues for their recommendations. Then, visit your local computer merchant and pick his or her brain about the best choices for you.

Choosing the Right Type of Internet Service

You have plenty of options when deciding upon your Internet service provider. New providers appear regularly, and each one has its own way of describing its services. Don't let the vast number of choices overwhelm you; in fact, there are only a few things you need to know to choose the right service. I'll describe them here, and at the end of this appendix I'll summarize them in a list of questions you can ask potential providers as you shop around.

► ► ► **A Note about Online Services**

Signing up with an online service such as America Online, CompuServe, or Prodigy is not the same thing as getting an Internet account. While some of the online services offer limited access to the Internet, most do not provide storage space on a Web server for your use. Those that do charge a premium for the service.

If you currently have an account with an online service, I recommend getting a separate account with an Internet service provider for the sole purpose of Web publishing. You'll have full access to the Internet, plenty of personal storage space on a Web server, and you'll be able to use state-of-the-art Web browsers and other Internet software.

► ► ► **Y**ou may already have access to the Internet through your work or university. Even so, as a Web publisher, you need your own private account for a couple of reasons. First of all, in addition to access, you need storage space on a Web server for your home page files. Chances are, your university or company won't readily allow you access to their servers. More importantly, most companies and universities have policies that restrict the use of their networks to official business. If your system administrator finds out that you're publishing a personal website using company/university equipment, you could be in hot water.

SLIP or PPP Connection

Most providers offer two types of accounts for the average home or office user: shell accounts and SLIP/PPP (Serial Line Protocol/Point-to-Point Protocol) accounts. To use Internet Assistant (and all of the other Internet software I talk about in this book), you need a SLIP or PPP account (preferably PPP). Without going into the nitty-gritty, a SLIP/PPP account gives you full access to the Internet using Windows' friendly graphical user interface. A shell account, while providing the same access, does so using a text-only, UNIX-based interface.

Full Internet Software Package

Your Internet account should come with a full suite of Internet software and easy instructions for installing it onto your computer (or better yet, an automatic installation program). The package should include:

■ *A TCP/IP stack:* Short for *Transmission Control Protocol/Internet Protocol,* this program allows your computer to be able to exchange information over the Internet.

■ *An e-mail program*

■ *A Web browser*

■ *An FTP program*

  ▶ ▶ ▶ **I**f your software package *doesn't* include all of the above programs, many are available for downloading over the Internet (you'll find links to many of the most popular Internet tools on the Online Resource).

Web Server Storage Space

In addition to a software package, your Internet account should include at least 10 megabytes of storage space on your provider's Web server (where you will be storing your home page files). If your website includes lots of graphics, sounds, or videos, you may want 15 megabytes or more, since these file formats quickly eat up storage space.

▶ ▶ ▶ **O**rganizations called *Web presence providers* offer storage space on their Web servers without giving you full access to the Internet. This is a cost-effective option for some, but if you're planning on getting involved with Web publishing, you need full Internet access.

Local Access Number

Make sure your provider has an access phone number (often called a *point of presence* or a *POP*) that's in your local calling area. When you connect to the Internet, you use your modem to "dial in" to your provider's servers. Essentially, your modem places a phone call to a modem connected to their computers. Once a connection is made, you can log onto the Internet. The last thing you want is for that connection to accrue long-distance phone charges.

Some providers have 800 numbers that allow you to dial in toll-free from anywhere in the country. This is a handy feature if you travel a lot, although you usually pay a higher rate to use it.

Services for Web Publishers

Look for special services for Web publishers, such as CGI scripting, logs that keep track of how many people visit your site (sometimes called *hit logs,* because they record the number of "hits" your site receives), and custom domain names. These services may cost extra but will be very useful as your Web publishing expertise grows and your website becomes more sophisticated.

▶ ▶ ▶ **C**GI scripts are discussed in Lesson 8, and domain names are discussed in Lesson 2.

Network Setup

You should inquire about your provider's hardware and network setup. Things to know:

- *User-to-modem ratio:* This is important because it gives you an indication of how busy the provider is. When you dial in to your provider, there needs to be an unoccupied modem on their end to answer the call and connect you to their servers. If all of the modems are already occupied by other users, your modem will go unanswered or will get a busy signal, and you won't be able to connect. This can be extremely annoying, especially if you have to wait a long time to log on. To avoid this, providers need to keep the user-to-modem ratio relatively low. A good baseline is one modem per twenty users.
- *Modem speeds:* Your provider's modems must be of the same speed or faster than yours. If the modem speeds are different, you will connect at the lower rate. For example, if you use a 28.8 modem, but connect to a provider who only has 14.4 modems, your Internet connection will only be 14.4. (The numbers here refer to kilobytes transferred per second.) Most providers accommodate modem speeds of at least 14.4, with many supporting 28.8 modems as well.
- *Backup procedures:* Internet service providers aren't immune to system crashes. For that reason, it is imperative that they have a consistent backup policy and procedure in place. After all, you store your home page files on their computers; the last thing you need is for your files to be wiped out by a system glitch.
- *System security:* Your provider should have someone on staff who is an expert in network security; a "hacker-guard," if you will. You should feel confident that a professional is in charge of keeping your information secure.

Responsive Customer Support

No matter how easy the Web is to use, you may find yourself in need of help from time to time. Your provider's customer service staff should be approachable, responsive, and knowledgeable. They should be reachable by phone and e-mail, and should respond to problems or questions promptly.

In addition to support, customer-oriented providers make other help resources available, such as internal "members-only" newsgroups (so that users can benefit from each other's experiences), online instructions for common tasks (such as uploading files to the Web server, changing your password, etc.), and an *FAQ list* (list of frequently-asked questions and their answers).

Cost

The cost for the kind of Internet service I describe above varies. Some providers charge a low monthly fee, with a per-hour charge for the time that you are connected. Others charge a higher monthly fee, with no connect charges. Still others charge a one-time setup fee when you sign up.

You should expect to pay somewhere in the neighborhood of $25 per month for 50 hours or more, and an initial setup fee of $30. You can find cheaper rates, but they may come at the expense of service and support (not necessarily, but it's something to keep in mind as you shop around).

Make sure to ask if the charges are the same if you publish a personal versus a commercial, or business, website. Some providers charge more if they think your site is a money-making operation or can be chalked up as a business expense. Also, ask if they charge higher rates for high-traffic sites. Some providers will make you pay an extra fee if your website consistently receives a high volume of visitors. Finally, ask how much they charge per megabyte if you find you need additional server storage space.

▶ ▶ ▶ I caution you against working with providers that attract you with low monthly fees, only to charge you for the hours you're online. You'd be surprised how quickly those hours add up, especially as you get more involved with Web publishing. I recommend paying a little more each month for the peace of mind that comes with not having to worry about how long you've been connected. Fifty hours per month (that's an hour and 40 minutes per day) is a good place to start.

Choosing an Internet Service Provider

Now that you know what you're looking for, it's time to start shopping around. Here are a few tips on how to find out about the Internet service providers in your area:

- Ask your friends for their recommendations. Word of mouth is often the most reliable source of information.

- Read your local or regional computer magazine (two popular examples include *Computer Currents* and *MicroTimes*). These magazines, available for free in many cities, include advertisements and articles about Internet service providers.
- Check with your local computer user groups for advice and recommendations. Many user groups have *SIGs* (special interest groups) devoted to Internet use and access, which are full of friendly advisors.
- If you have Internet access though your work or school (or if you can borrow a friend's account for an evening), there are some excellent resources available on the Web. One is the ever-helpful Yahoo, with links to the home pages of providers all over the world. Another is called the List, and it is single-mindedly devoted to indexing Internet service providers. The List is handy because you can search by geographical location, by area code, by name, and more. I've included links to both of these websites in the Online Resource.
- When shopping around, call a selection of local *and* national providers. National providers service the entire country, and often other countries as well. Local providers, while they serve a smaller geographical area, often have a more personal touch, as well as a devoted community of users.

Summary: A List of Questions

Here's your shopping list. Once you compile a list of prospects, call them and ask the following questions, and then compare the results.

  If you have Internet access, a lot of this research can be done online. Most Internet service providers' home pages answer some or all of the questions below.

- Do you offer SLIP/PPP Internet accounts?
- Do your accounts come with a software package? What programs does it include?
- Do your accounts include Web server storage space? If so, how much space?

- Do you have a local access number? Do you have a toll-free (800) access number?
- Do you offer services for Web publishers such as hit logs, CGI scripting, and custom domain names? How much do you charge for these services?
- What is your user-to-modem ratio? Do users often get busy signals when trying to log on?
- How fast are your modems?
- Do you have a backup procedure in place?
- How do you ensure that your network is safe from hackers?
- What are the hours of your customer support staff? Do you provide other help resources for your users?
- How much does an account cost? Is there a setup fee? Are there per-hour connect charges? Do you have different rates for personal versus commercial websites? Do you charge more for high-traffic sites? How much does extra server storage space cost?

► ► ► I can't stress enough the importance of a positive "gut feeling" when choosing your Internet service provider. You should feel good about the people with whom you choose to work (this is a partnership, after all). If, when you call, you feel you are being patronized or made to feel that your questions are foolish, strike that provider from your list and move on!

Once You've Made the Choice

Once you've settled on a provider, you're ready to go. If you find that you use your Internet account a lot, you may want to consider installing a second phone line just for your modem. That way, you'll be able to leave your telephone free for callers, and you can websurf and publish to your heart's content.

If you find after a time that you are dissatisfied with your service, be sure to speak up. Send a brief note to the support staff, explaining why you are dissatisfied. Most Internet service providers appreciate the feedback and will work with you to solve the problem. If, after that, you *still* don't get the service you expect, don't hesitate to refer to your notes and switch providers.

Appendix B

Installing Internet Assistant

Everything you need to follow the examples in this book—Microsoft's Internet Assistant software, sample HTML documents, graphics, sound, and video files— is contained on the CD included here. This appendix gives you step-by-step instructions for installing Internet Assistant on your computer (you'll be happy to know that it practically installs itself).

Internet Assistant requires 4 megabytes of hard disk space to be able to function. Make sure that you have at least that amount free before you install it onto your computer.

 ▶ ▶ ▶ **I**f you received Internet Assistant as part of a software bundle, the installation instructions are different (but still intuitive and very easy). See the Online Resource for details.

To begin the installation process, make sure that your CD-ROM drive is turned on, Windows 95 is running, and that all other software programs are closed.

 ▶ ▶ ▶ **I**f you downloaded Internet Assistant from Microsoft's Internet site, you can still use these directions; just locate the Internet Assistant setup file on your hard drive and start from there.

1 Insert the CD into your computer's CD-ROM drive.

2 From the desktop, double-click on the **My Computer** icon.

▶ A window opens and displays the folders and drives on your computer.

3 Double-click on the **Cd-rom** icon.

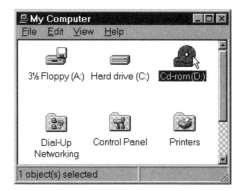

▶ A window opens and displays the contents of the CD. *wrdia20z.exe* is the name of the Internet Assistant setup program.

4 Double-click on the **wrdia20z.exe** icon.

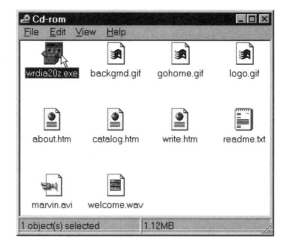

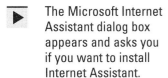

The Microsoft Internet Assistant dialog box appears and asks you if you want to install Internet Assistant.

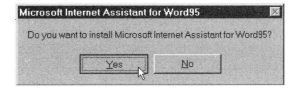

5 Click on the **Yes** button.

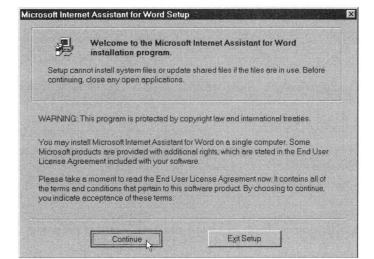

A status bar appears indicating that the Internet Assistant files are being *extracted,* or restored to full size after being compressed to fit on the CD, then the Microsoft Internet Assistant for Word Setup dialog box appears. It asks you to close all open applications (you already did before we began the installation process) and to read the End-User License Agreement.

6 Click on the **Continue** button. (If you would rather install Internet Assistant later, you can click on the Exit Setup button to return to your desktop.)

There is a short pause as Setup examines the contents of your hard drive to see if a previous version of Internet Assistant is already there.

▶ The End-User License Agreement appears. This is your contract with Microsoft that specifies how you may lawfully use the Internet Assistant software.

7 Read the agreement. When you reach the end, click on the **Accept** button.

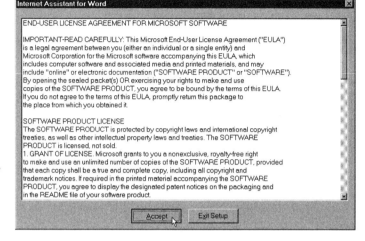

▶ The Microsoft Internet Assistant for Word Setup dialog box appears.

8 Click on the large square button to do a complete installation.

▶ The Setup program checks that you have the necessary disk space and installs Internet Assistant onto your computer. It creates a new folder within the Program Files folder on your hard drive called Internet Assistant, and stores all of the files there.

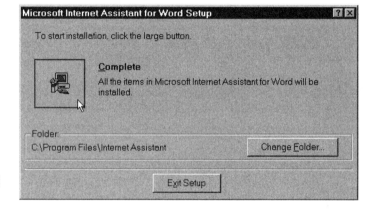

▶ When installation is complete, a dialog box appears telling you Internet Assistant setup was completed successfully.

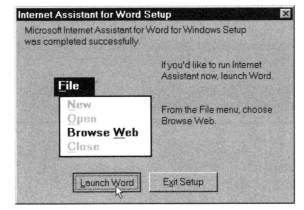

9 Click on the **Launch Word** button to launch Microsoft Word (or, if you'd rather wait to get started, click on the Exit Setup button to return to your desktop).

Congratulations...you are now on your way to becoming a Web publisher! Lesson 1, "Getting Started," will introduce you to the world of Web publishing and show you how to start using Internet Assistant.

▶ ▶ ▶ If you decide you would like to remove Internet Assistant from your system, you can do so easily by using the same Setup program you used to install Internet Assistant. Open the Setup program and continue through its steps until you reach the Microsoft Internet Assistant for Word Setup dialog box. Click on the Remove All button, and the Setup program will remove all of Internet Assistant's files from your computer.

INDEX

Note to the Reader: Boldfaced numbers indicate pages where you will find the principal discussion of a topic or the definition of a term. *Italic* numbers indicate pages where topics are illustrated in figures.

U

V

END-USER LICENSE AGREEMENT FOR MICROSOFT SOFTWARE

IMPORTANT—READ CAREFULLY: This Microsoft End-User License Agreement ("EULA") is a legal agreement between you (either an individual or a single entity) and Microsoft Corporation for the Microsoft software accompanying this EULA, which includes computer software and associated media and printed materials, and may include "online" or electronic documentation ("SOFTWARE PRODUCT" or "SOFTWARE"). By opening the sealed packet(s) OR exercising your rights to make and use copies of the SOFTWARE PRODUCT, you agree to be bound by the terms of this EULA. If you do not agree to the terms of this EULA, promptly return this package to the place from which you obtained it.

SOFTWARE PRODUCT LICENSE

The SOFTWARE PRODUCT is protected by copyright laws and international copyright treaties, as well as other intellectual property laws and treaties. The SOFTWARE PRODUCT is licensed, not sold.

1. GRANT OF LICENSE. This EULA grants you the following rights:

- **Installation and Use.** You may install and use an unlimited number of copies of the SOFTWARE PRODUCT.

- **Reproduction and Distribution.** You may reproduce and distribute an unlimited number of copies of the SOFTWARE PRODUCT; provided that each copy shall be a true and complete copy, including all copyright and trademark notices, and shall be accompanied by a copy of this EULA. The copies may distributed as a standalone product or included with your own product.

2. DESCRIPTION OF OTHER RIGHTS AND LIMITATIONS.

- **Limitations on Reverse Engineering, Decompilation, and Disassembly.** You may not reverse engineer, decompile, or disassemble the SOFTWARE PRODUCT, except and only to the extent that such activity is expressly permitted by applicable law notwithstanding this limitation.

- **Separation of Components.** The SOFTWARE PRODUCT is licensed as a single product. Its component parts may not be separated for use on more than one computer.

- **Software Transfer.** You may permanently transfer all of your rights under this EULA, provided the recipient agrees to the terms of this EULA.

- **Termination.** Without prejudice to any other rights, Microsoft may terminate this EULA if you fail to comply with the terms and conditions of this EULA. In such event, you must destroy all copies of the SOFTWARE PRODUCT and all of its component parts.

3. COPYRIGHT. All title and copyrights in and to the SOFTWARE PRODUCT (including but not limited to any images, photographs, animations, video, audio, music, text, and "applets" incorporated into the SOFTWARE PRODUCT), the accompanying printed materials, and any copies of the SOFTWARE PRODUCT are owned by Microsoft or its suppliers. The SOFTWARE PRODUCT is protected by copyright laws and international treaty provisions. Therefore, you must treat the SOFTWARE PRODUCT like any other copyrighted material.

4. U.S. GOVERNMENT RESTRICTED RIGHTS. The SOFTWARE PRODUCT and documentation are provided with RESTRICTED RIGHTS. Use, duplication, or disclosure by the Government is subject to restrictions as set forth in subparagraph (c)(1)(ii) of the Rights in Technical Data and Computer Software clause at DFARS 252.227-7013 or subparagraphs (c)(1) and (2) of the Commercial Computer Software— Restricted Rights at 48 CFR 52.227-19, as applicable. Manufacturer is Microsoft Corporation/One Microsoft Way/Redmond, WA 98052-6399.

LIMITED WARRANTY

NO WARRANTIES. Microsoft expressly disclaims any warranty for the SOFTWARE PRODUCT. The SOFTWARE PRODUCT and any related documentation is provided "as is" without warranty of any kind, either express or implied, including, without limitation, the implied warranties or merchantability, fitness for a particular purpose, or noninfringement. The entire risk arising out of use or performance of the SOFTWARE PRODUCT remains with you.

NO LIABILITY FOR CONSEQUENTIAL DAMAGES. In no event shall Microsoft or its suppliers be liable for any damages whatsoever (including, without limitation, damages for loss of business profits, business interruption, loss of business information, or any other pecuniary loss) arising out of the use of or inability to use this Microsoft product, even if Microsoft has been advised of the possibility of such damages. Because some states/jurisdictions do not allow the exclusion or limitation of liability for consequential or incidental damages, the above limitation may not apply to you.

MISCELLANEOUS

If you acquired this product in the United States, this EULA is governed by the laws of the State of Washington.

If this product was acquired outside the United States, then local laws may apply.

Should you have any questions concerning this EULA, or if you desire to contact Microsoft for any reason, please contact the Microsoft subsidiary serving your country, or write: Microsoft Sales Information Center/One Microsoft Way/Redmond, WA 98052-6399.

About This CD

This CD-ROM contains everything you need to follow the lessons in this book, including Microsoft's Internet Assistant software, HTML files you will use to build your home page, and graphics, sound, and video files you will use to brighten it up.

FILE NAME	WHAT IT IS
wrdia20z.exe	Microsoft Internet Assistant software
about.htm	HTML file
catalog.htm	HTML file
write.htm	HTML file
logo.gif	Graphic file
gohome.gif	Graphic file
backgrnd.gif	Graphic file
welcome.wav	Sound file
marvin.avi	Video file
readme.txt	Explanatory text

About the Web Publishing Online Resource

There are gigabytes of information about Web publishing available on the Internet, with something new appearing every day. I've collected the most helpful tools and tips together in one place: the *Web Publishing Online Resource.* Once you've created a home page using the examples in this book, you can use the Online Resource as your base to further explore the world of Web publishing.

Here's a sample of what you'll find:

- Late-breaking news about Internet Assistant
- The latest HTML tags and extensions
- Web browsers and Internet software to download for free
- Clip art galleries
- Tips on home page design
- Usenet newsgroups devoted to Web publishing discussions
- Web search utilities that will help you find whatever you're looking for
- Internet service provider directories
- Tips on how to publicize your website
- And much more!

  The Web Publishing Online Resource is located on the Web at **http://www.dnai.com/webpub**.